Praise for *The Jewish Way to a Good Life*

"Rabbi Shira has written a beautiful book for anyone interested in learning about Judaism, or hoping to enrich their own daily Jewish experience, and she does it as only she can: with humor, joy, sensitivity, and a foot each in the ancient and modern worlds."
—Joshua Malina, actor and cohost of *The West Wing Weekly*

"Rabbi Shira makes Judaism feel alive, relevant, and totally accessible. If you're Jewish but haven't been able to find your way in, she holds the door open for you. If you're not Jewish and want to live with more meaning and joy, she welcomes you. You'll feel lucky to have her wise and encouraging voice in your head for years after you read it."
—Hanna Rosin, host of *Radio Atlantic* and author of *The End of Men*

"As a Muslim, I found much-needed hope, guidance, and practical advice in Rabbi Shira Stutman's *The Jewish Way to a Good Life*, in which she generously shares her community's wisdom and traditions for a universal audience. This book, born from warmth and kindness, is the sermon we always wanted in Sunday school: inviting, nonjudgmental, uplifting lessons on how we can build resilience, empower our communities, tolerate our obnoxious family members, and resolve to live a life of purpose and empathy."
—Wajahat Ali, author of *Go Back to Where You Came From*

T0361616

The
**JEWISH
WAY**
to a
**GOOD
LIFE**

The
JEWISH
WAY
to a
GOOD
LIFE

Find Happiness,
Build Community, and
Embrace Lovingkindness

RABBI SHIRA STUTMAN

THE EXPERIMENT

NEW YORK

The Experiment, LLC
220 East 23rd Street, Suite 600
New York, NY 10010-4658
theexperimentpublishing.com

THE EXPERIMENT and its colophon are registered trademarks of The Experiment, LLC. Many of the designations used by manufacturers and sellers to distinguish their products are claimed as trademarks. Where those designations appear in this book and The Experiment was aware of a trademark claim, the designations have been capitalized.

The Experiment's books are available at special discounts when purchased in bulk for premiums and sales promotions as well as for fundraising or educational use. For details, contact us at info@theexperimentpublishing.com.

Library of Congress Cataloging-in-Publication Data

Names: Stutman, Shira, author.
Title: The Jewish way to a good life : find happiness, build community, and
    embrace lovingkindness / Rabbi Shira Stutman.
Description: New York, NY : The Experiment, [2025] | Includes
    bibliographical references.
Identifiers: LCCN 2024058504 (print) | LCCN 2024058505 (ebook) | ISBN
    9798893030174 | ISBN 9798893030181 (eBook)
Subjects: LCSH: Jewish way of life.
Classification: LCC BM723 .S76 2025 (print) | LCC BM723 (ebook) | DDC
    296.7--dc23/eng/20250103
LC record available at https://lccn.loc.gov/2024058504
LC ebook record available at https://lccn.loc.gov/2024058505

ISBN 979-8-89303-017-4
Ebook ISBN 979-8-89303-018-1

Cover and text design, and cover illustration, by Beth Bugler

Manufactured in the United States of America

First printing March 2025
10 9 8 7 6 5 4 3 2 1

To Suzanne, Ned, and Jon, on whose shoulders I stand.
To Caleb, Ma'ayan, and Natalia, who inspire me to be better.
And to Russell, whom all of this is for.

Contents

The Way of . . .

I want to tell you a story.

It was the beginning of the Jewish holiday of Yom Kippur and the synagogue was packed. (Actually, we were not in the literal synagogue. We had rented a Baptist church because so many wanted to attend services that evening that we needed more space than usual.) People were settling in for a two-hour prayer service. Yom Kippur is one of the holiest days in a Jewish calendar filled with holy days. For twenty-five hours, some Jews neither eat nor drink. The main goal of the holiday is to look backward and apologize for last year's missteps, and look forward and set intentions for the year to come.

Standing on the pulpit, looking out at the congregation, I recognized many of the faces: people who over the past year had lost loved ones or had a new baby; who had graduated from or been kicked out of a PhD program; who found out they had cancer or were in remission. They had brought their heavy loads, their great blessings, and their banal, day-to-day lives to services that evening.

There also were the great many who were not regular synagogue attendees, whose faces and stories I didn't know. They looked at me with hooded eyes—or, more likely, looked down at their phones. A lot of them expected exactly nothing from that evening. Their lived experience of Jewish prayer services was that they were boring or irrelevant. Like many others, they went to synagogue for Yom Kippur reflexively, out of a sense of obligation to their ancestors or their spouse. The service hadn't even started, but already they couldn't wait for it to be over.

I felt the weight of the moment. I chose to be a rabbi because I truly believe that religion—that Judaism—can help us lead deeply meaningful lives. It can inspire and push us to be the best version of ourselves.

How could I translate this love to those sitting in front of me? What tools did I have that could provide support, inspiration, love, and—for those who need an extra push—challenge?

The service began.

We removed the Torahs from the ark. Three people stood on the pulpit, holding them, and representing the full community. They are a physical representation of the fact that as we enter the sacred holiday and prepare to do the incredibly difficult work of *teshuvah*—finding the best parts of who we are and who we can be—we are not alone. There are others who will walk with us on this journey.

When Jews use the word "Torah," we may be referring to a few different things. There are the "Five Books of Moses"—Genesis,

Exodus, Leviticus, Numbers, Deuteronomy—which are the first part of the Hebrew Bible. Sometimes we expand the definition of the word "Torah" to include a wide swath of sacred Jewish teaching throughout the millennia. When I use the word "Torah" here, I am talking about the scroll, calligraphed in black ink on parchment sheets sewn together, from which Jews read a weekly portion at services four times a week and on holidays.

The Torah scroll is both an object itself and a surrogate and symbol. It represents the Jewish reverence for education. It is a reminder of all that Jews have sacrificed over the millennia in defense of our tradition. One of the scrolls being held that evening, for instance, had survived the Holocaust, being found under the floorboards in a home in Europe, hidden there as the home's occupants were taken to the concentration camps. It is called "a tree of life" because, like many trees, it has deep roots and is a constant presence.[1]

Torah has endured for thousands of years because it is the origin story and launching pad for Jewish teachings about justice, holiness, compassion, and community. These teachings morph and evolve depending on the era in which we live, but they also hold certain core truths. I may teach different passages of Torah in 2024 CE than my ancestors did in 24 BCE, but I am teaching from the same text. We return to the foundational texts so as to build upon them, adapting to the pressures and blessings of the current moment.

That evening at Yom Kippur services, as the prayer called Kol Nidre was being recited, with the Torahs lovingly held (I can't remember by whom) on the *bimah* (platform), I made a split-second decision. I thought to myself: How can we embody the idea of a strong and enduring Torah? How can we connect Torah to all of the beauty and challenges of the contemporary messy, chaotic American Jewish community?

In a few chapters, you will read about the Jewish approach to the body. (Spoiler alert: It is a favorable one.) We are an embodied people. Much of our spiritual practice happens with our spirits *and* our bodies. I therefore decided at that moment that, after we finished the Kol Nidre prayer, instead of putting one of the Torahs back in the ark, we were going to pass it around the room, from person to person, each one getting the opportunity to hold it.

Over the course of the rest of the evening, I watched as the Torah moved through the sanctuary and people held it. Some cried, and some couldn't get rid of it fast enough. For some, it was the first time they had ever held the Torah. Some were Jewish, and some were not. Everyone got an equal chance. Once they held on to the Torah, what they did with it was up to them. Judaism was truly in their hands.

It is a perfect encapsulation of what I'm trying to do with the book you are holding right now: give you a tiny piece of Torah in the hopes that it can help you build a life of meaning, and when the time is right, you will pass it on.

This book is different from other introductions to Judaism because it encourages anyone, Jewish or not, to take on some of our traditions, which are meaningful enough to have stood the test of time. For most of our history—and for reasons stemming from Jewish law to antisemitism to the fact that Jews represent only about 0.2 percent of the world's population[2]—our texts and traditions were most likely known and observed by Jews only. For a non-Jew to take on a Jewish-themed Shabbat practice (or mindfulness-based eating practice) would have been viewed as farcical or even offensive. But one of the blessings of twenty-first-century globalization is that it allows us entrée into other cultures and traditions. You no longer have to *be* Jewish to *do* Jewish. All are welcome in our community of practice.

About 1,800 years ago, a rabbi called Rav was part of a conversation about what it means to live a good life.[3] He and five of his colleagues each had a prayer that they would recite a few times a day, an indicator of their goals for a life well lived. Each of the rabbis' prayers was slightly different, but each was a meditation on the fact that a meaningful life does not happen *to* us; we have to make it happen ourselves. We set goals and then keep them in the front of our minds as we work to achieve them.

The fact that more than a half dozen rabbis' prayers were listed in one of our sacred texts is a reminder that a "meaningful life" may look different depending on where and when you live, your culture or socioeconomic status, your race, ethnicity, sexual orientation, or religion. The book you are about to read was written through the lens of my own bias and privilege. The core issues that I seek to address involve questions around rest (we work long hours and do not take many vacations), inequity (our society continues to struggle with racism and economic inequality), and community (our civic infrastructure—from church, synagogue, and mosque attendance to political engagement—is breaking down). If I were living in a different time or place, or had other life experiences, my own search for meaning might look quite different.

There is no universal definition of a meaningful life, but Rav's personal prayer became the basis for a communal prayer that we recite before the beginning of the new Jewish month. In this prayer we ask that, in the month ahead, we find joy, and feel or bring upon ourselves a life of blessing. We ask for a long, healthy, and peaceful life filled with goodness. We commit to trying not to do anything that would require rebuke, and to operating from an abundance mindset, pursuing honor and not shame. We want to continue learning and fulfill our goals.[4]

Today, as in the first century CE, one of people's most basic needs is to create a meaningful life. We want to know that our time on this Earth matters, that we will leave our corner of the world a little bit better than we found it. Research indicates that 57 percent of Americans ask themselves at least once a month how they can find more meaning and purpose in life, with 21 percent saying they consider the question daily or weekly.[5] We are a meaning-seeking species.

Reflecting on my thirty-year career as a rabbi and educator, I recognize that part of what gives my life meaning is learning about Judaism and then translating that learning to all sorts of people—Jewish or not—who are curious and open. Judaism is a meaning-making technology that can help people lead more purposeful lives. Somewhere in these pages is a tradition that can help you grow, change, and connect more deeply with others. This is true whether you are Jewish or atheist, Christian, Muslim, Hindu, or pagan, or practice any one of the more than four thousand world religious traditions. You can hold on to this tradition, and you can pass it on.

Judaism is not unique; there are sparks of meaning making and meaning building in every culture, religion, or spiritual practice. I love Judaism because it is mine; I want to share it with you because perhaps it is yours, or because one of the sparks will speak to you and help you make and sustain a change in your life.

Judaism was never meant to be lived in the home or synagogue only—it was meant to be lived with every single breath you take. On the street, in the store, or in your place of work, each of these locations are prime places to put what you will learn in this book into action. If you take the sparks of holiness from most faith traditions—I happen to know Judaism, it happens to be mine—they can help elevate all of your daily acts, from the way you commute in the morning to how you treat the people you see when you're waiting at the bus stop, from whether to compost or recycle to the way that you behave in the office or in your business.

It shouldn't only be Jews who get to benefit from Jewish practices. Over the course of my career, I have been lucky that the communities I have served have been composed of Jews and many "Jewish-adjacent" folk. These are the people of other or no faith tradition who are related to Jews or who are spiritual seekers who want to learn from all traditions. They have been invited to life-cycle events such as weddings, baby namings, or coming-of-age ceremonies. Whenever I lead a Jewish service, give a talk, or conduct a ceremony, my working assumption is that at least a third of the people in attendance are not Jewish.

This is a new experience in Judaism. For the majority of Jewish history, Jews either lived separately from those who were not Jewish, or at the very least had restrictions on the ways the two groups interacted. Antisemitic policies and our own provincialism kept us from having certain types of careers, attending universities, or otherwise integrating into the larger society. It was not until the last few hundred years that many Jews began to have the opportunity to work with, live near, become friends with, or even marry people who were not Jewish. In my opinion, while there are definitely losses associated with assimilation, on balance we have gained more than we have given up.

Judaism is not a closed tradition—many of its practices are open to anyone, Jewish or not. Deciding not to engage in commerce one day a week and calling it the Sabbath is a practice that is open to everyone. Eating ethically is open to everyone. Giving our money to those in need is open to everyone. Communities need boundaries, but dividing the world into "insiders" and "outsiders" can sometimes be unnecessary and even dangerous. A lot of "what Jews do" is as accessible, relevant, and useful to people who are not Jewish as it is to Jews.

I want you to learn more *about* Judaism, but I don't care at all whether you *are* Jewish or become so. We Jews are not much interested in proselytizing because we do not believe that non-Jews are going to hell. Over the course of our history, so many Jews have been forced to convert to other religions on pain of torture or death that the whole concept of proselytizing feels icky at best, dangerous at worst.

This book contains some of the best of what Judaism has to offer. Unfortunately, I could write a whole other book about Jewish teachings that are sexist, homophobic, and xenophobic. Our tradition is ancient; Jews have lived all over the world and metabolized some hateful ideas. And if I am being totally honest, some of the hurtful teachings are original to us, as well. We, too, have our own bigotries. In opening the doors of Judaism wide for everyone, my hope is that this book is a type of *tikkun*, a type of repair. Contemporary Jews and fellow travelers can simultaneously lift up the positive core values in our tradition and provide redress for the hurtful ideas.

This should not be difficult. From its earliest days, the Jewish tradition has made an art of continually evolving. After being expelled from our homeland in 70 CE, Jews have lived all over the world, often learning and borrowing from the cultures in which we lived, shifting and expanding our theology and practice. Some traditions have been maintained (Sabbath, for instance), and some have not (animal sacrifices). Sometimes we end up with two traditions that stand at odds or in conflict with each other, but both stand! (Some Jews eat corn and rice on Passover, and some do not.)

Judaism has a few orienting principles that will resurface throughout the book both obliquely and explicitly. For instance, Jews believe that our behavior in *this* world matters, and that we have the agency, ability, and responsibility to make a difference. The world *as it is* is not the world *as it could be*. We believe that ideas and emotions are natural and good, and should be expressed. And we strongly prioritize showing up for each other—when times are difficult, when they are joyous, and for every moment in between. Look for these principles throughout the book, whether we are talking about love and sex, mourning, or learning. They are the threads that weave the Jewish people together.

Even though 27 percent of Jews profess to be atheists,[6] God is ever present in Jewish text and tradition. It is my working assumption that many readers of this book will, themselves, be atheists. And this is fine. I don't care at all whether you are a believer, but I include "God talk" because it is sometimes helpful to understand a people's theology in order to understand and learn from its culture and tradition. To you atheists and agnostics out there, it might be helpful to insert the words "the universe," "the good," or "unlimited potential" every time I mention the word "God."

It is also critical to understand the Jewish concept of *mitzvah*, or "commandedness," the core belief that God demands certain actions and ways of being in this world. Mitzvot include welcoming the stranger, honoring the elderly, and not taking revenge. The 613 mitzvot in the Jewish tradition are just the beginning of the tens of thousands of laws in the Jewish legal tradition, often called *halacha*. A mitzvah is a discipline, not an option; a requirement, not an offering of the heart. Humans have free choice, but some Jews accept the mitzvot as a whole piece, not just those that resonate for us at any given moment.

This book is intentionally set up differently from other introductions to Judaism; it contains a buffet of options from which the reader can pick and choose. It also contains maybe 0.5 percent of all the laws associated with any one subject. Perhaps that fact may inspire you to further exploration. At the very least, it is important to understand that for some people, Jewish practice only makes sense as a *system*; teasing it apart to choose one law or another is akin to dropping random letters out of words in a sentence and expecting it to make sense. It's possible, but more difficult.

Much of this book was written in early 2024, in the shadow of the war between Israel and Hamas. Like many American Jews, I felt powerless to stop the devastation of a land I love so much, and the terror and deaths of so many who live between the Jordan River and the Mediterranean Sea. Since October 7, 2023, I have alternately felt like I was awaiting an imminent death or in mourning; I have felt proud and ashamed; I have been an atheist and a believer. Writing this book has been a balm in an incredibly difficult time.

Over these last years, and especially over these last months, as I watched antisemitism tick up in the United States, I thought often of the winter of 1993 on the campus of Columbia University. There, a small group of Jewish students started an organization called Lights in Action, with the goal of fighting antisemitism by promoting Judaism. After I was summarily kicked out of the election for president of the Jewish Student Union (a story for another time), I became part of the group, and felt that, Jewishly, I went from black-and-white to technicolor. Even though I have been called a "labrador puppy for Judaism," I am not naive; I know that dangerous, evil antisemites exist. Fighting those groups and ideas is not my work in the world, however. My work is to lift up the fact that religion can be a source of good, that Judaism is a wellspring of compassion, intellectual growth, connection, creativity, and hope.

Three times a day in Jewish prayer services, traditional Jews ask that the words we say and the prayers we offer be acceptable to

"You."[7] Of course, the "You" in this line, from the biblical book of Psalms, is meant to be God. In Judaism, every single human being was created in the image of God, and we have the spark of the divine within us. As I offer this book to you, then, I ask that the divine spirit in each of us be able to learn something from this offering of my heart.

Chapter 1

The Way of *Chesed*: Acts of Lovingkindness

hesed is one of the most foundational of all Jewish values.[1] Like many Hebrew terms laden with history and human experience, it is difficult to translate in just a word or two. So permit me thirty: Chesed happens when someone takes notice of another being, often one in a moment of suffering or vulnerability, and does something kind or loving to help alleviate pain or disequilibrium.

Chesed is more than "love" because you do not have to love—or even know—the person or people you are serving. It is not just "kindness," because it is a verb in addition to a noun, and because it involves the "courage and imagination" it takes to step into daunting spaces and do the hard work of caring and the even harder work of doing it well.[2] Chesed is an act of showing up in a world in which too many of us are—or feel—unseen.

Some of the specific acts of chesed mentioned in traditional Jewish texts are as follows.

- Providing clothing to the needy
- Visiting the sick
- Honoring one's parents
- Making peace between people
- Caring for a corpse before burial
- Comforting mourners

These acts are so critical to us that there is no limit to how often we can be asked to do them, nor how great the reward.[3] Thousands of actions fall under the heading of chesed, depending on the people we are trying to serve. The Jewish charge is for each of us to move closer to the ideal of embracing chesed as both a posture and a practice, doing as many acts of chesed as possible.

Why do chesed?

For the last few years, I have been a volunteer with Court-Appointed Special Advocates (CASA), helping to support a young person in the foster care system. In Washington, DC, where I live, the CASA program is always desperate for volunteers. In some ways, the work has been inspiring. The young woman I accompany, Rachel, has overcome more than most. (While this story is entirely true, many of the details have been changed to protect Rachel's privacy.) She was abandoned by her mother at a young age, then adopted, then placed back into the foster care system by her adoptive parents when she reached adolescence. Rachel has ADHD, dyslexia, and other significant learning differences. When she gets angry, she loses her temper completely and often destroys property, which has gotten her kicked out of many foster homes.

Acts of chesed, large and small, make Rachel feel not as alone. Sometimes one of the staff members in her group home will drive her to Walmart so she can buy something to make her drab room a little more beautiful. I will bring my dog Boaz to visit Rachel because he gives her comfort. I can tell her that one of her former social workers speaks with me when I need advice on how to navigate a complex, bureaucratic, and sometimes heartless system.

Chesed breeds chesed. Last December, Rachel found a broken Christmas tree discarded on the street, brought it into her foster home, propped it against the wall to keep it (somewhat) vertical, and decorated it for everyone's enjoyment. All of these moments of chesed happened because each of us noticed the suffering of another, and then did something to alleviate it. Rachel said that it was her thank-you to her foster mother, who had done something kind for her.

How do you begin? You begin

Because the actions that fall under the heading chesed are so many and so diverse, starting a chesed practice can feel overwhelming. There will always be sick friends, hungry people on the street, young people who could benefit from a mentor, or mourners needing to be comforted.

I'm reminded often of Loren Eiseley's essay "The Star Thrower," in which a boy walking on a beach after a storm sees many starfish scattered along the shore. Starfish out of water soon die, so the boy picked up starfish after starfish, flinging them into the sea to save them. For every starfish he threw back into the sea, another one would wash up on the shore. An adult saw the boy attempting this Sisyphean task, and chided him. "For every one you save, another one returns. If you can't save them all, why bother trying?" The boy looked at the starfish in his hand, and retorted, "It matters to this one." Then he returned it to its home.

I'm continually inspired by this story. It gives me strength when people tell me that I should not bother to help Rachel, whether it's because there are just too many youth in the foster care system or because my advocacy has not been as transformative as I would have hoped it would be.

With my help, is Rachel a happily employed high school graduate? She is not. She struggles every single day. As I write this sentence, she is unemployed. I am not optimistic about Rachel's ability to secure full-time work. I still believe that every act of chesed matters.

I try not to judge others. Really. But when it comes to chesed, and to my work with CASA, I find certain kinds of responses frustrating. People say, "Oh, you're a CASA? I would never have the time." Or "I would not know what to do." Or my favorite: "I would care too much." These disappointing statements reflect certain assumptions about me and this work.

- There is some magical amount of time that is "enough."
- I have specific skills in caring for youth in the foster care system.

- If I am not doing everything in my power to help this person, it is as if I am doing nothing at all.

None of these is true. I had set my mind to doing more chesed in this world, and I decided to do it through the CASA program. Here I am now, fumbling along the best I can, giving as much time as I can. Am I the best CASA volunteer in the history of CASA? Nope. Am I doing my best? Most of the time. Am I making a difference in Rachel's life? Yes.

There is a reason that there are so many clichés about "taking the first step," including my favorite: "Do not let the perfect become the enemy of the good." Cynicism, fear, self-centeredness, and anxiety keep us stuck in one place, and we make excuses for not doing the next right thing. We think that because we cannot make a significant dent in this broken world, we shouldn't bother to try to help anyone. We worry that if we start to care a little, a dam will burst and we will become overwhelmed by caring too much. Worst of all, given that the human capacity for dissociation is stronger than many of us realize, we may not even notice how often we choose to just look away.

To these challenges, I offer the theologian Anne Lamott's story of her little brother's elementary school project. In her extraordinary book *Bird by Bird*, Lamott writes of a time when her ten-year-old brother was desperately trying to finish a school report on birds. He was given three months to write the report but had procrastinated; the report was due the next day. "He was at the kitchen table close to tears," Lamott writes, "surrounded by binder paper and pencils and unopened books on birds, immobilized by the hugeness of the task ahead. Then my father sat down beside him, put his arm around my brother's shoulder, and said, 'Bird by bird, buddy. Just take it bird by bird.'"[4]

I think of this story—and of the starfish—every day. When it comes to chesed, I do what I can, while always pushing myself to do a little bit more. Right now, I have a cousin who just learned she has cancer; I have not called her. One of my best friend's children is in the hospital; I am bringing her dinner tonight. One of my friend's marriages is teetering; I spent a lot of time on the phone with her last week, just listening. A former congregant's partner is sick; I respond to every single text they send, no matter what time. A dear friend's child is having a baby-naming ceremony; I will not be there to celebrate with them. Yesterday, someone on the street asked me how to get to the nearest drugstore; I stopped, pulled out my phone, and showed them on a map. My daughter wanted a ride to school; I told her that she should walk because I wanted to exercise. I am doing my best.

"You are not required to complete the work," reads one famous Jewish teaching, "but neither are you free to desist from it."[5] "The world is built with chesed," explains another.[6] How is the world built? Brick by brick, say the rabbis. Or bird by bird. Ancient rabbis teach that taking small steps of chesed and other acts of service is the most important principle in Judaism.[7]

Chesed looks different for every person. One person's easy, fun act of chesed is another's hardest. As you begin a chesed practice, lean into what you already love doing. If you are a good cook, cook for families with a new baby or who are going through a difficult time. If you love to party, celebrate a bride or groom by dancing with them, singing for them, or writing a poem for them at their wedding. If you are really organized, help someone who needs their home cleaned out. If you're a big talker, visit with someone you know is lonely.

"Fun" chesed is only the beginning. Continue to push yourself toward acts of chesed that are less enjoyable and even quite difficult. Remember those who are truly suffering, and for whom it is objectively more difficult to show up, including the socially awkward or people who are sick or dying and those who care for them. Excuses I have heard about why people don't visit the sick include "I don't know them well enough." Why people don't spend time with a developmentally delayed child so a parent can get a break: "I would not know what to say." Why a person wouldn't help a friend who has a broken arm with their garden: "I have a brown thumb." The problem with these excuses is that they center *you*, and not the person who would be on the receiving end of your act of kindness. I have never heard a mourner complain because someone they didn't know well showed up for a visit during their time of mourning. I have never heard a parent of a developmentally delayed child refuse to give advice to a caretaker about how best to interact with the child. While I have been at the hospital and witnessed patients tell visitors, "Now is not a good time," those patients still appreciate that someone showed up for them. Begin with what is easy, one step at a time. Never stop moving forward.

Some people are reluctant to engage in chesed because they worry about a power disparity or a perceived sense of pretentiousness associated with believing that you can help someone else. Who am I to think that I can make Rachel's life any better? Who are you to think that so-and-so even *wants* a visit from you? This becomes especially true when our acts of chesed are toward someone from an oppressed or marginalized group with less power or influence than you have. While we should examine our reasons for engaging in acts of chesed, the true image of chesed is less noblesse oblige and more "We've all been there" or "This could have been me." It's less hierarchical—as in the mighty caring for the disempowered—and more familial in nature.

Sometimes people ask for an act of chesed that we cannot provide. If you cannot do exactly what a person asks, that doesn't mean that you are free to do nothing. Consider what happens when people on the street beg for money. You may choose not to give because you give charity elsewhere. You may refuse because you fear that the money will be used for illegal drugs (which is probably untrue, as only a quarter of those who beg are addicted to illegal drugs).[8] You may be annoyed because you think that beggars are "clogging up the sidewalks" in unsightly ways. Maybe you do not have any cash on you. I, too, have thought of all these reasons. I then remind myself that interacting with people who beg is an opportunity for chesed. Even if you are not going to give money, you can humanize this person in front of you, recognizing that they are unique and holy, and not entirely different from you or people you love. Humanizing may be as simple as looking a person in the eye when they ask for money, even if your response is "Not today." Sometimes, you might offer a granola bar or a fast-food gift card that you have with you. Acts of chesed remind us that every human being has an inherent dignity.

Chesed sometimes even happens reluctantly. You are standing in the security line at the airport, and someone asks if they can cut in front of you because they are about to miss their flight. You can say, "Of course!" and step aside, or you can say, "You shouldn't be so irresponsible," roll your eyes, and step aside. Both are acts of chesed. But which response would feel better for the recipient—and for you? The next time you are going through your closet or pantry to give clothes or food to those in need, it may be tempting to think, "If someone is cold enough, or hungry enough, they will wear/eat whatever I give them." That may be true, but it is ungenerous in a way that undermines the definition of the term "chesed." When you clean out your closet, put aside clothing that is too stained to be worn. Make sure that what you donate is clean and folded, so that the people who sort the clothes will have an easier time and the recipients will feel a sense of dignity when receiving one of your old garments. It is a double act of chesed to be concerned not only with the end-wearer of your clothing but also with the workers who organize and transport your clothing to its new home.

In Judaism, it is acceptable to do the right thing for the wrong reason. Letting someone cut in front of you in the security line at the airport because you feel shamed into it still gets the person to their gate on time. While everyone would feel better about a chesed interaction that begins with an open heart, your resentment is not an excuse not to be generous.

What happens when we try but mess it up?

A few years ago, the "paying it backward" trend, in which a person at a coffee shop or fast-food restaurant would pay for their order and then the order of the person behind them, gained some traction. The goal was to see how many people, finding out that someone had paid for *their* food or drink, would then pay for the person behind *them*. Sounds lovely, no? Chesed.

One day, I walked into a coffee shop and after I had purchased my coffee turned to the man behind me and said, "I'd like to buy you coffee as well." It was a disaster. The man didn't speak much English and didn't understand what I wanted from him. No problem, I thought. I speak passable Spanish, the language in which he was berating me, saying, "I don't need anyone to buy coffee for me! I can buy my own coffee!" I tried to explain, "No, esto es una idea que aprendí en el Internet para ser amable con otras personas. Se llama 'pagar al revés.'" (This is an idea I learned on the internet to show kindness to other people. It's called "pay it backward.") He was infuriated and continued to insist that he didn't need my "charity." I thought about pulling out my phone to show him videos of people "paying it backward" but decided I should cut my losses. I apologized profusely, got my coffee, and left the shop.

That was a tough one.

When I got back to my car after the interaction at the coffee shop, I was shaking. I was embarrassed, which made me angry. How *dare* the man not accept my act of chesed? How *dare* the person who stood behind the counter, and who also spoke Spanish, not help me translate? Didn't they know that I was just trying to do good?

Luckily, I had a long drive ahead of me, enough time to realize that sometimes the most difficult part of chesed is that we so want to be acknowledged or rewarded for our acts that we forget we are a kindness *facilitator*, not the main character of this drama.

"Main Character Syndrome" (MCS) happens when we see ourselves as the protagonist in every situation. While it is understandable to center yourself in the narrative of your own life, one question to consider when embarking on an act of chesed is: "Who am I doing this act *for*?" How am I enacting the core Jewish value of upholding human dignity? Instead of offering to pay for coffee for the man behind me, I could have taken the three extra dollars I would have spent and put it in the tip jar for the coffee shop workers, who make minimum wage. I could have turned to the man behind me and said, "Good morning, how are you?" to get a sense of him. I could have bought a coffee shop gift card to give to the next person I saw begging on the sidewalk.

When we do acts of chesed, we may not get it right. The best way to learn how to do this work well is just to do it. We learn through trial and error. When we make mistakes, as we undoubtedly will, we hope that those we offend have chesed themselves and understand that we are trying. Chesed isn't expected only of the best of us; it's expected of all of us.

Is chesed a purely selfless act?

Some argue that acts of chesed should be purely altruistic. We should attend a funeral, welcome guests into our home, or help someone cross the street with zero expectation of reciprocation.

Judaism tends to be more realistic about human nature, under-standing that the majority of human beings do not behave purely altruistically. We are motivated by a desire for acknowledgment, an alleviation of our own shame around our privilege, the hope that whatever goodness we do to someone else is done back to us, and many other reasons.

There are no saints in Judaism.

When we do an act of chesed, we are, in a sense, making a deposit in the "mitzvah bank." While there is not a one-to-one correspon-dence between the goodness we put into the world and the good-ness that is done for us and to us, Judaism understands our acts of chesed as part of a larger ecosystem.

The term "chesed" is technically a noun; when we want to make it a verb, we talk about "gemilut chasadim." ("Chasadim" is the plural of the word "chesed.") The first word of this phrase, "gemilut," is colloquially translated as "acts" but actually means "*reciprocal* acts." As Judaism understands it, when we do an act of chesed, the *energy generated by that act* will make the world better in a way that will benefit us. You generate a "credit," not just for you but for the whole world.

Selflessness is doing good without expectation of recompense. Gemilut chasadim is doing good because the more acts of chesed you do in the world, the better the world will be overall. Whatever you do is for the good of humanity, including your own self.[9] Some rabbis argue that we do good in this world because there is—just maybe—a heaven in which it matters how we behaved during our time on Earth. *All* rabbis agree that we do good because it creates a virtuous cycle here in our lifetime.[10]

Science supports the not-purely-altruistic approach to chesed. Some benefits of doing acts of kindness include the following.

- Increased self-esteem
- Improved mood
- Decreased blood pressure and cortisol
- Longer life
- Increased sense of connectivity with others
- Boosted levels of satisfaction and well-being[11]

Being kind, which is one part of chesed work, literally changes the brain. Chesed toward others is a form of chesed toward oneself, with one exception: chesed shel emet, or the chesed of truth/ eternity. This is the specific act of caring for a dead body up until the time that it is buried. This is the highest form of chesed because there is no reciprocal act associated with it; the dead cannot do chesed anymore, not for the people who care for them nor for anyone else.

Where chesed ends

Is there such a thing as too much chesed? For the majority of us, this is not an issue. Most of us need to find ways to do *more* chesed in this world, not less. For the few who do and give too much, this is for you.

In Judaism, chesed does not stand alone. It is often paired with its counterpart, din: strict judgment. Consider the parable of a ruler who had her best glassblower fashion two cups from extraordinarily delicate glass. The ruler realized that if she poured boiling water into them, they would expand and burst. If she froze the water in the cup, it would contract and break. Instead, she mixed hot and cold water, and poured them into the cups, and they did not break.[12]

I cannot attest to the science of this parable, but its moral is strong. If we live in a world in which we do chesed 24-7, we will not have energy, time, or space for our own needs. This is the world of Shel Silverstein's *The Giving Tree*, in which the mighty tree ends up as a stump because all it does is give to others, without allowing itself to grow or flourish in any way. Perhaps you know someone—it may be you!—who gives so much that there is nothing left. This can be exhausting for them, as well as for their family members.

There are limits to chesed (or, in rabbinic parlance, "corrupted chesed").[13] We need boundaries to protect ourselves from giving so much that we harm ourselves or the people we are trying to help. In those moments, we have to actualize the value of din. The first time I called Rachel, she was surprised to hear from someone she didn't know and said terrible things to me. I got off the phone with her (din) but encouraged her to call me back when she was ready to talk (chesed).

Sometimes acts that we call chesed are actually self-serving or harmful to the person we are trying to help, especially when it comes to family. Consider young children who refuse to go to sleep, and who hour after hour, night after night, ask for "one more kiss." It is chesed to walk into their room and give them extra kisses so they can settle into sleep more peacefully. At a certain point, the effect on you of lack of sleep—and the effect of your frustration at the situation—will overtake the abundance of acts of love. Even in the most difficult situations, however, and even as you protect yourself or your loved ones from people who are quite needy, there can still be sparks of chesed.

I believe we live in a moment when the attribute of din is more fully developed than the attribute of chesed. We often assume the worst of others, and not the best. When someone tries to cut us off on the highway, instead of letting them in (chesed!), we become infuriated and drive faster to get ahead of them "because we were there first." A friend asks you to help her move and you say no because she was not available to help you when you moved last year. We become infuriated with customer service representatives about issues over which they have no control under the assumption that "they are *all* responsible for this screw-up."

If any of the above describes you, try to do it differently. In most cases, erring on the side of chesed will usually do you (and the world!) more good than making the mistake of strict judgment.

I love doing acts of chesed, but I hate receiving them

Several years ago my daughter Ma'ayan had brain surgery. There's one moment from that time that I've been turning over in my mind ever since. It was a tiny moment, maybe thirty seconds. Ma'ayan wasn't even present. It was a few months after the surgery and Ma'ayan had returned to school. I was speaking to the mother of one of her school friends. I mentioned the surgery, and the other mother looked surprised.

"Oh, did you not know that Ma'ayan had a *smidge* of brain surgery?" I said. This was a glib way I often described what the neurosurgeon did. In the surgery, he had placed electrodes throughout my twelve-year-old daughter's brain, then cut through the muscles near her shoulder to implant a battery, which she would wear for the rest of her life. Just a smidge.

She looked at me curiously, as if I were a smidge delusional. "Yes, Shira, I knew," she said. "Everyone knew; Ma'ayan was out of school for six weeks. We were all thinking about you, but we didn't reach out, because we know how private you are. We wanted to bring you meals but thought you wouldn't want us to intrude."

That line: *How private you are.* I am many things, but "private" is not one of them. I scoffed at their comment—clearly they didn't really know me—and moved on in the conversation.

If I'm not private, then why didn't my family and I reach out to the community for support? Why didn't we ask for a meal train? Why didn't we ask for chesed, the way we had done for others? Why did we choose to be so damn quiet about the whole thing?

In ancient times during the holidays, hundreds of thousands of Jews made the pilgrimage to the Temple in Jerusalem. It was a joyous time, during which pilgrims made offerings: of the first fruits of the trees, of the first lambs and calves, of the barley or wheat harvest. Three times a year, everyone was required to appear and bring their own gift.[14] But "appearing" meant showing up in a very particular way. It is *not* private, *not* walled-off. It is mutual and messy. There is no limit to how often we can perform acts of pilgrimage and gift-bringing, nor to how great the reward is for doing so. Good news, considering that there were hundreds of thousands of people in the Temple during these pilgrimage festivals.

Maybe there is something that we should have done differently in the lead-up to or the aftermath of Ma'ayan's surgery. Even today, though, I still balk at the idea of requesting chesed. How can I ask already busy families to make and bring us food that we could easily order ourselves? We had excellent health care, I was able to work part time for six weeks to care for my daughter, and this amazing, life-changing surgery didn't even *exist* twenty years ago. We were luckier than most. Did I really deserve chesed?

A number of years ago, Rabbi Sharon Brous taught me an extraordinary text from the ancient complication of laws called the Mishnah. In the ancient temple, pilgrims would circle to the right—except for "those to whom a 'thing' had happened," like a mourner, or someone who was ostracized from their community. Those people (the ones in pain) would circle to the left. Others would see them and ask, What happened to you? Those circling to the left would have to answer. In the midst of the joy of pilgrimage, sadness and pain were not only *permitted* to exist; they were *spotlighted*. Those who were hurting could not hide. They had to walk in the opposite direction from everyone else to emphasize just how outside the typical frame of reference they were at the time. The text doesn't indicate what that "thing" is, only that it affected someone enough that they experienced the pilgrimage differently than most others did. While everyone else was heading in one direction, they were heading in the other, symbolizing their pain in a moment that for other people is filled with joy. The moment of interaction is both an individual *and* a communal response to suffering; do not suffer alone.

Where might your reluctance to allow others to care for you come from? In an uber-capitalist United States, which has an individualistic mindset based on the entirely false and dangerous premise that we are not interconnected, we may be confused, thinking that *our* behavior somehow does not impact our neighbors. The fundamental truth of chesed teaches that we *are* interconnected. My choice to buy an electric car instead of an SUV *does* affect other human beings. My family's unconscious decision not to ask for help *affected others*. We did a disservice to ourselves *and* to the community by keeping them at arm's length.

We have internalized the distorted belief that leaning too much on others is a sign of weakness. Perhaps my reluctance to talk about Ma'ayan wasn't about protecting my family's privacy but instead about protecting the image of our family as strong and able to handle everything.

What if we flip the script, defining "strong" as allowing ourselves to be fully cared for in our realness, in our pain? What if the term "self-reliant" became more of an insult than a compliment? What if, when we were "the ones to whom something had happened," it was our *responsibility* to walk counterclockwise and allow ourselves to be taken care of? We are interconnected; we have a duty to each other. In Judaism, "pilgrimage," or spiritual growth, is done not as a solo endeavor but in community. Our pain does not belong just to us. I wish we could see that as a relief and not a burden, a kind of strength to help us in our complicated lives.

Whatever pain we have needs to be let out. If we try to hide it away, it may come out in other ways, such as treating people poorly, ignoring our health, or as shame. Our pain doesn't go away unless we express it and receive support.

It can be exhausting to receive gifts—food or kind words—from others. When we are struggling with our own emotions or with the practicalities surrounding illness, we may feel that we don't have anything left to give. To those already depleted by life, I offer a word of caution: Accept others' offerings with grace, for them and for you. Allow yourself to take the risk of being seen and held.

There is a teaching that when the Jews went on pilgrimage to Jerusalem, every single person, hundreds of thousands, fit into the Temple at the same time.[15] How wonderful that all could participate in seeing each other! We are also taught that there was enough room so that each person had four cubits (roughly six feet) around them at all times. Allowing yourself to be cared for is not synonymous with baring your soul all the time, everywhere. If and when you need it, create and cultivate a circle of quiet in a sea of holy chaos.

Whether we are receiving or giving, it's not clear who is gaining more. During the ancient pilgrimage, the relationship between high priest and pilgrim was more symbiotic than solitary. Who, after all, was the receiver—the high priest, who led the people but was reliant on their offerings of food, or the pilgrim who fed the spiritual leader physically, but was nourished by him spiritually? The one to whom something has happened receives the support of the one who asks after them. The one who offers their care, their service, will also be less lonely, more connected to others, and will feel the

joy that comes from giving of themselves to build a more meaningful world. Each person comes with their own gifts. Practice giving
and receiving those gifts.

Chapter 2

The Way of
Ahava: Love + Sex

When you search the phrase "V'ahavta—love your neighbor as yourself"[1] from the biblical book of Leviticus, you get more than 110 million hits on Google. It makes sense, given that this is one of the most well-known lines in the Hebrew Bible. But what does it *mean* to love another person? What does it mean to love yourself?

In Judaism, the verb "to love" is, like many verbs, an action word. In the words of Rabbi Angela Buchdahl, love "is a verb here in the Torah. 'V'ahavta' is in the command form: 'You shall love.' Which is kind of an amazing thing—because how can you command a feeling? Well, you can command the loving action. I think too often we think of love as this ephemeral emotion, but our tradition values action more." On its own, love is like an uncooked cup of noodles;

love can *exist* between people even if not acted upon, but it's an ineffectual and poor attempt at nourishment. It's not until you add the boiling water that the noodles become a meal of sorts. Love, too, becomes sustaining only when it is activated. We may deeply care for other humans, or even for ourselves, but if we don't do anything to act upon this feeling, then love is impotent. When the Israelites accepted the Torah at Mount Sinai, our tradition holds that they said *na'aseh v'nishma*—we will do and only then will we comprehend. There is a sense that *acting* out of love brings love. Sometimes we must do the action even *before* we can feel the love.

While the *feeling* of love may be universal, the types of people with whom you share your love are not. In this chapter, we will begin with self-love, understanding that "love your neighbor as yourself" by definition implies that you love yourself first. We will then talk about platonic, romantic, and erotic love, and finish with love of the stranger. There is overlap in the Venn diagram of these types of love but significant differences in how they are expressed.

You can only love your neighbor as much as you love yourself

I once had a congregant named Tabitha who often sought me out after Shabbat services for the sole purpose of denigrating and gossiping about other people. A fellow congregant was appointed to a new job; Tabitha wanted me to know that this person only got the job because of connections. Someone showed up at services looking fabulous; Tabitha would comment derisively about their weight. Without any sense of irony, she would even complain about how awful it was that certain other congregants tried to share gossip with her!

As someone who has struggled to avoid gossip myself, I found being around Tabitha quite difficult. At first, whenever she would start talking about someone else, I would just stay silent and hope she would stop, with little success. One day I was speaking with a colleague about Tabitha (there I go, gossiping!) and she said, "Isn't it terrible how much Tabitha hates herself?" It was the clearest of light bulb moments. Perhaps Tabitha was vicious to others because she was vicious to herself. If she could learn to love herself, maybe she would learn to love others as well.

If this hypothesis is true, in order to take seriously the instruction to "love your neighbor as yourself," we have to begin with you. Since gaining this insight about Tabitha, I set an intention that whenever we were together and she started slandering others, I would change the subject to . . . Tabitha! She might say, "Wow, look at how awful that person's outfit is!" and I would say, "Tabitha, tell me about something good going on in your life," or "Did I ever tell you how grateful we were for those delicious cookies that you shared with our staff a few weeks ago?" I tried to lift her up in the hopes that it would make her feel good about herself. The perhaps odd or improbable hypothesis was that a person who likes and is proud of herself will not feel the need to denigrate others in order to make herself feel better. Whenever Tabitha—or anyone else who spent a lot of time gossiping—started up with vicious gossip, I would try to change the subject to them. This strategy stops the gossip about 75 percent of the time. I also hope it helps them love themselves more.

Self-love sometimes gets a bad rap, because people incorrectly take it to mean self-centeredness, which *is* a problem. Recognizing that you bring something special to the world is appropriate[2]; expecting the world to revolve around you 24-7 is not. Self-love means appreciating your own self-worth and paying attention to your own well-being, which is quite different from narcissism.

Working toward self-love is critical for a number of reasons. Consider the "Tabitha principle": It is easier to care for others when you first care for yourself. You were born with as much dignity as every other human being. You are deserving of love and happiness! And research proves that having a sense of self-love makes us happier.[3]

But globally, one third of humanity struggles with self-acceptance and self-value. More than 60 percent of American women report having negative thoughts about themselves daily.[4] And suicidality increases among those who do not have a sense of self-love.[5] We have a lot of work to do to help human beings achieve a feeling of self-worth.

For some people, loving *others* is easy; it's loving *oneself* that is difficult. How do we begin? Start by trying to change the story you tell yourself about how you show up in the world.

There's a story I tell myself from time to time: I fear that my mom thinks that I am a terrible daughter. It makes me like myself a little less. I worry that I don't see her enough, I don't take her to doctor's appointments, I don't . . . massage her feet? What is it that my mother wants or needs, exactly? I don't actually know, because I've never asked her.

Do you also have a story that you tell yourself that keeps you from loving yourself? We're not alone. Consider the ancient Jewish tale of twelve scouts sent into the land of Canaan to explore in advance of the Israelites' settling there. Ten came back convinced that the Israelites would not be safe in the land. These scouts said that, compared to the inhabitants of Canaan, they felt like grasshoppers, and that everyone they met perceived them as grasshoppers. Two scouts, Caleb and Joshua, returned and said the land was "flowing with milk and honey"[6] and that the Israelites would be happy there. The fearful voices of the ten drowned out the brave voices of the two, and the Israelite community became hysterical with fear.[7]

The rabbis teach that God was furious at the ten scouts because they made assumptions about the Canaanites. "How could you possibly know what they thought about you?!" God fumed. "Maybe they thought you were actually there to help the community!"[8]

I have compassion for the scouts, who had recently been freed from slavery in Egypt and were now wandering through the desert in search of home. They must have felt unloved. How might the Israelites have behaved differently if they thought that the Canaanites saw them as partners rather than as lowly grasshoppers? How might I feel differently if I saw myself as a *great* daughter rather than as an inconsistent or inattentive one?

The fallible, very human Israelites of thousands of years ago are no different from many of us today. I have found myself imagining others having certain thoughts about me, not because they actually *did* have those thoughts, but because *I* felt a certain way about myself. It's a terrible, vicious cycle. *I* feel like a bad daughter, so therefore my mother must think I'm a bad daughter. I then get mad at my mother because how dare she think that I'm a bad daughter! My mother becomes an avatar onto whom I project all of my emotions. I choose to believe something that leads me to like myself *less*, instead of changing my behavior or asking the person most impacted what they think. It's not so different from Tabitha.

One of the foundations of healthy relationships is not only *knowing* our feelings, fears, and vulnerabilities but also coming to peace by appreciating and even loving them. The Israelites and scouts were not able to grow in this way. They were stuck in a destructive mindset, refusing to do the work to see themselves—and therefore others—differently. They considered themselves to be grasshoppers. They assumed everyone agreed.

Even as the global self-love movement reached a $9.6 billion valuation in 2018,[9] I am not convinced that self-love is something you can buy. Instead, it's something you build. Try spending more time with people who see you as lovable and worthy of love. Ask them what they like or love about you. If you find yourself trying to downplay what they are saying, ask yourself, "What would it mean if this were true?" If it is true of that person's opinion of you, with enough practice it could become your opinion of yourself.

For those of you who are parents, if you cannot love yourself just because it's the right thing to do for *you*, then think about your children. Model self-love because it may help your loved ones live longer and happier lives. If you can look at someone else—anyone else—and think easily to yourself, "That person deserves love, no matter what they do in the world," try to metabolize that emotion and turn it toward yourself. Every human being has something lovable about them, even the smallest spark. Recognize that in yourself; it will help you do more good and be more kind to yourself and to others.

"Better than even the love of women": platonic love

After the death of his best friend, Jonathan, in battle, King David said that their love was "better than even the love of women."[10] David and Jonathan were living representations of the Hebrew word *chaver*, which means "friend" but also "attached together." They were best friends in life, and David mourned Jonathan deeply in death. Their relationship is a reminder that while building and maintaining close friendships is not easy, it is one of the most important things we can do to lead a meaningful life.[11]

While some people choose to believe that the love between David and Jonathan was romantic, I choose here to see it through the lens of platonic friendship, which is no less important. Rabbi Avigayil Halpern commented to me about this story: "Many readers—especially queer readers—see romantic and not platonic love between David and Jonathan in these texts. This is a powerful site of seeing one's own identity and experience reflected in text—*and* we can always read Torah in multiple ways! Additionally, in queer community, the lines between close friendship and romance are often blurrier, making this distinction somewhat artificial."

"Friendship" in the Jewish imagination has a specific definition. Chaver, like so many Hebrew nouns, is an action word. It describes a relationship in which the participants help each other be better and do better. The most honored friendships are like "iron sharpen[ing] iron,"[12] exemplified by those who do not shy away from voicing their strong opinions and in so doing strengthening each other. (There is a special way that iron encounters iron in order to sharpen it; there are certain skills that friends should use when they exchange sharp opinions.)

We learn, "Any love that is not accompanied by reprimand is not [true] love."[13] Friends love, but they also challenge. People are considered actual friends when they are able to both correct each other and receive feedback when they have misstepped. When two or more people are true friends, what is created between and among them is different from whatever could be created by each of them on their own.

Judaism has many suggestions for how to maintain friendships. Friends share sit-down meals together, understood as a social activity and an opportunity for learning. Friends are people with whom we share our secrets.[14] Friends have sleepovers, because sometimes the best secrets come out late at night, and sometimes it can take a whole evening to work through a disagreement or a difficult subject. Friendships do not begin in a vacuum, nor are they maintained in one.

A "friend" maintains a deeper level of intimacy than a coworker, neighbor, or someone who is just a member of one's community. Robin Dunbar, an evolutionary psychologist at the University of Oxford, teaches that the average person is able to maintain about fifty "good friends." Given the depth of friendships according to Jewish tradition, that may feel like a lot of people. Whatever number is right for you, however, understand that having friends who are "like family," who may be closer to us than our own family of origin, is desirable and normal in Judaism.[15]

The fierceness of romantic love[16]

In Judaism, romantic love is not ephemeral. It is grounded in the ups and downs of long-term partnerships. This teaching is evidenced by the ketubah, the marriage contract couples sign at their wedding. The ketubah clearly lays out many of the spouses' expectations for one another. The traditional ketubah emphasizes four areas in which partners have responsibilities for each other. Partners must do the following.

1. Make sure that their partner has enough food to eat
2. Make sure that their partner has enough clothing
3. Have sex with their partner (the number of times a week depends on the work that each partner does in the world)[17]
4. Provide for alimony in case of divorce

This list may feel random to the contemporary eye: Why clothing and not housing? But the intent is just as important today as it was almost 2,500 years ago, the date of the earliest surviving ketubah.[18] A ketubah can serve as the springboard for conversations about how to be in a long-term romantic relationship with another person. What do you pledge to provide to each other? Jewish tradition forgoes platitudes such as "caring" and "honor" for practicalities such as cooking and saving for retirement. Don't just *say* you love me, Judaism teaches: *Show* me you love me every single day.

In the spirit of intellectual honesty, one more word on the ketubah. In the ancient ketubah, and even today in certain communities, the commitments made are not mutual. The traditional text is entirely heteronormative, placing the male partner in the role of protector/owner. The female is basically silent, having been "acquired" by the male; only the male can divorce the female. The ketubah paradoxically is also a proto-feminist document that provides protections for the wife that were unavailable in other ancient Near Eastern cultures. The rabbis who crafted the earliest ketubahs could not have imagined the egalitarianism that we experience or fight for today. Given that the ketubah has always been an attempt—however flawed from a contemporary perspective—to protect the rights of women, I think the traditional ketubah is ripe for reinterpretation.

As in platonic friendships, Judaism teaches that romantic partners show love not by placating their partner but by challenging each other when appropriate.[19] Having lively conversation, even including respectful disagreement, is a key part of a healthy partnership. Maintaining peace in the home is a core Jewish value[20]; so is being a formidable interlocutor. Your life partner should inspire you to build a better world not only in your own home but also at work and in your community.[21]

Even those of us who deeply love our romantic partners sometimes have moments when we are too harsh or too subdued during difficult conversations. With that in mind, whenever I start wedding planning with a couple of any age or stage, I tell them that they should have a couples counselor on the proverbial speed dial.

A counselor can help you process and learn from communication gaps, in the hopes of avoiding these same pitfalls in the future. Skilled, transparent communication is foundational to a partnership in which couples challenge each other with love and respect. The modern Jewish cultural appreciation of therapy represents an acknowledgment of how objectively complicated relationships are, how there are nadirs for everyone, and how communication that is curious, humble, reflective, and nonreactive can help partners zero in on and smooth down their own rough edges, thus gaining a better understanding of what they can realistically give to their relationships.

"Kiss me with the kisses of your mouth"[22]: sex

Looking for some hot erotica? Consider the Bible! The biblical book Song of Songs is filled with verses extolling the gorgeous sexuality of the human body.[23] It talks about kissing and touching, lust and love. The ancient rabbis attempt to explain the erotic imagery by insisting that the sexual relations described in the book are not between humans but instead are metaphors of love between the Jewish people and God. Even if that is true, it means, in the words of Rabbi Avigayil Halpern, "The rabbis think God is sexy, and that overlaps with thinking sex is sacred and good." The ancient rabbis "eroticize Torah as an indicator of the way that Judaism truly reveres eros."

Judaism is pro-sex within the bounds of a monogamous, committed relationship, and in some other contexts. Sex is not just for procreation but also for physical pleasure. Rabbis extoll not only the type of sex that might lead to pregnancy but also foreplay of all sorts. A rabbi named Nachmanides teaches that we should "first introduce the mood with" words that evoke "passion, closeness, love, will, and erotic desire. Then seduce your partner and do not hurry in arousing passion." In a heterosexual relationship, the man is supposed to make sure that his female partner reaches orgasm first.[24] We see reference to consent, seduction, and other sex acts. Permission is NOT given to have sexual relations with someone against their will, even if you are married to the person.[25] Sex is not just an animalistic act. Intimacy is critical.

There is a well-known story in the sixth-century set of legal texts known as the Talmud about a student who wanted to learn the teachings most central to Judaism. What did he do? He went and hid under his teacher's bed while the teacher and his wife were "taking care of their needs," which is a euphemism for having sex. They weren't only engaging in physical sex acts; they were also chatting and joking with each other.[26] The student was surprised. "This couple has been together for so many years," he thought aloud, "and they are as enamored of each other as if it were the beginning of their relationship!" Note here the interplay between the physical and the emotional; in Judaism, they cannot easily be separated.

The story concludes with the teacher hearing the student musing to himself. The teacher furiously kicks him out of the room, because of course what the student was doing was voyeuristic and forbidden. The student's invasion of the privacy of his teacher and the teacher's wife's was unacceptable. As Rabbi Avigayil Halpern writes, "Talking about sex is both welcomed in the proper time and places and also a topic around which we can ask for privacy."

This story teaches that intimacy between partners, even after many years of partnership, is not only desirable but is a critical Jewish teaching. Partners should be attentive to each other's desires and needs, whether they have been together for one year or for sixty.

Ancient practice, new meaning: menstruation and intimacy

The ancient practice of *niddah*, in which partners do not engage in sexual intimacy if one of them is menstruating, has disappeared in many Jewish communities. People deem it heteronormative or sexist in origin and application and object to niddah's depiction of menstrual blood as "impure." While all of that is true, one could argue that in getting rid of the entire practice of niddah, we are throwing out the baby with the bathwater. This ancient tradition has a number of lessons for today that teach us how to be in a deep and long-lasting relationship, even if there are no menstruating people in the relationship, and even if we do not precisely follow the traditional rules.

Niddah reminds us to set structure and clear expectations in our relationships, and to respect each other's bodily needs. There are some couples who, many years after they first meet, still have a mutually enjoyable and regular sex life. Their sex drives match and they love how their bodies look, neither one ever claiming to "have a headache" to get out of having sex. For the rest of us, however, who may experience a growing sense of sexual dullness over the course of a lifetime, who may have a decreased sex drive, or whose life may be filled with distractions and the ever-expanding responsibilities of the world, setting expectations around sexual intimacy can be helpful.

Given the pressures of the rest of life, and given each partner's sex drive, how many times a week should couples have sex, and when should it be?[27] Some people don't find it romantic, but I often encourage couples to make "sex dates," so that each partner knows the expectations and can prepare by, say, taking a bath or a nap, making sure the kids are occupied or asleep, watching pornography, or whatever else it takes to become aroused. On the "off days," partners are free to yearn for each other in a way more akin to their first days of dating than to their twentieth year of marriage. Having days on which you know in advance that you will or will not have sex encourages partners to maintain a type of intimacy based not only on a particular sex act like intercourse but also on foot massages or love letters. Or perhaps even doing chores around the home, which many people find very seductive.[28]

Niddah reminds partners that even as they are committed to each other, and in some ways complete each other,[29] they are also separate individuals. If there are some days during the month in which couples do have sex, and others when they do not, then they are not at the whims of their partner in the same way as if there were no boundaries. This is especially true when there is a couple with mismatched sex drives—which is the majority of couples, in my experience as a rabbi who has counseled hundreds of couples. When sex is on or off the table at set times, for the partner who has a higher sex drive, there's something to eagerly anticipate, and for the one with a lower sex drive, there isn't the constant worry that they are not living up to expectations, or that their partner is going to pressure them into having sex when they don't want it.

The contemporary application of the ancient laws of niddah brings us back to a major theme of this book: Strong relationships require strong communication, both in bed and out of it. Be on the lookout for shame around sex, which many of us have unknowingly absorbed from family, religion, and society. Sex is meant to be fun and liberating, not shameful or painful. Sexual shame can lead to sexual dysfunction, loss of desire, fear of sex, or other illnesses. Shame around sex can create a vicious cycle in which one avoids sex because of shame, which only intensifies the shame, which leads to avoiding sex even more.

One of the blessings of a long-term partnership is that you have the opportunity to experiment and learn what you like sexually and what you do not. In Judaism, sex is encouraged throughout a lifetime, with no necessary connection to procreation. So do whatever it takes to keep the spark alive, including using sex toys, role-playing, reading or listening to erotica, watching some forms of pornography, or other methods for increasing sexual pleasure, as long as it is consensual.

Casual sex

What if, like so many people, you are reading this book while not in a long-term relationship? Does Judaism have anything to say to you about your sex life? Judaism embraces rather than rejects the physical, including sex. Almost all Jewish communities and rabbis today, myself included, will tell you that this sex-positive orientation applies mostly to committed monogamous relationships. Jewish texts do imagine sexual situations and experiences outside of committed monogamy, however, and have wisdom to offer there as well.

One ancient text[30] offers us a shocking story of rabbis—yes, rabbis!—having one-night stands. Whenever the second-century sage Rav came to the city of Darshish, he would announce, "Who will be mine for the day?" Whenever the third-century sage Rav Nahman came to the town of Shekhantziv, he would announce, "Who will be mine for the day?" The story suggests that these rabbis, traveling for their work, would seek out one-night sexual companions.

Later commentators, clearly troubled by this story, suggest that the invitation was always for temporary *brides*! The rabbis were asking who wanted to marry them and then be divorced the next day. What this spin tells us is that no traditional Jewish reader of the story could imagine rabbis having sexual relationships, even very brief ones, without a framework of accountability or responsibility. These rabbinic commentators imagine short marriages as the loophole to allow for one-night stands, but today we understand that there are other ways to maintain Jewish values in even noncommitted sexual encounters.

To bring a Jewish sensibility to casual sex is to act with the knowledge that every person we interact with is holy and a full person, not only a body or a means to our own pleasure. It means asking questions about desires and preferences and sharing about our own. It means openly discussing contraception and boundaries. Judaism teaches that we are accountable to one another—especially when we make ourselves as vulnerable as we do during sex.

An important note on queerness in Torah, contributed by Rabbi Avigayil Halpern

One verse in Leviticus has caused tremendous harm to humans in the Western world—both emotional and physical. For those of you not carrying the "ouch" of this text so deeply that you immediately know the verse, here it is: "Do not lie with a male as one lies with a woman; it is a *toevah*." I've left toevah untranslated here; it's been translated along the lines of "abhorrence" or "abomination," and it certainly means something bad.

There are so many questions that a careful reader can ask about this verse and its history of interpretation. There's no denying that historically in Judaism and Christianity, it is used at its most awful to support conversion therapy, and in its more gentle but still horrifying guises to forbid specific queer sex acts. There are other ways to interpret this verse, however. Judaism has a long history of what Rabbi Danya Ruttenberg has termed "textual activism": A key part of the ways Jews have always interpreted Torah is bringing our own values and experiences to reading it in ways that are creative and liberatory. The best way to think about queerness and Judaism in interaction is not as a problem at all, but as a thrilling opportunity. Queer Judaism is thriving, and it is contributing to a richer and deeper Judaism for all.

Queer wedding ceremonies are rites where couples and scholars explore how to formalize commitment without hierarchy. Queer yeshivas ("places of sitting") are opening new ways for all Jews to study our sacred texts. Queer Jews' courageous and life-filled engagement with our tradition is making Judaism better for us all. Let's celebrate this gift!

Loving the stranger

The root of the Hebrew word *ahava* (love) is *hav* (give). Love means giving.[31] The ancient rabbis remind us that there is only one biblical injunction to love your neighbor as yourself, but thirty-seven commandments to love the stranger. Rabbi Jonathan Sacks teaches that this is because it is easier to love our friends and neighbors because they are probably more like we are. "The stranger," he teaches, "is one we are taught to love precisely because he is not like ourselves."

Or are they? I sometimes think we are commanded to "love the stranger" not because they are *different* from us, but because we are more similar than we would like to think, and this makes us uncomfortable. I may feel that undocumented immigrants waiting at the border to enter the United States are entirely different from me by virtue of their religion, nationality, language, skin color, and, most important, legal status. However, only two generations earlier, *my* family were the immigrants, *my* grandparents the ones who neither spoke English nor understood American culture. This stranger is not so strange after all.

In Judaism, there is more than one way to enact love of a friend or family member but only one way to manifest love of a complete stranger, someone you will never meet, and that is through pursuing acts of justice. Will Herberg teaches that "justice is the institutionalization of love in society." He invokes the teaching of the theologian Martin Buber by arguing that we need to treat every individual, including the stranger, as a *Thou*, "a person, an end in themselves, never merely as a thing or a means to another's end."[32]

We love the stranger not in a conceptual way but in an action-based one. We will discuss this more in the chapter on *tzedek*.

Hate

Here's one way to bring more love into this world: Begin by hating less. "Do not hate your family member in your heart," one text teaches, understood as the inverse of "love your neighbor as yourself."[33] Ancient rabbis were quick to point out that this text did not say "never hate," because that would be impossible. It did not say "turn the other cheek," because human nature makes that difficult for the majority of us. The text commands us to recognize and acknowledge that we have these negative feelings, and to talk to the person who harmed us.

We don't have to waste energy hating someone; we can work on repair and moving on. Let the person know that you are hurt, and invite them to repair what has been torn. When someone does something terrible to us, we are taught to "rebuke them and say to them: 'Why did you do this to me?' Perhaps they did not intend what you think, or it was an accident."[34] Having fleeting feelings of hate is understandable; allowing the hate to lodge in your heart is not.[35] Some rabbis argue that *not* telling someone that they have hurt you is a sign of hatred![36] Maybe there is an explanation for their behavior, in which case you would be hating for no good reason.

Why aren't we commanded to love our parents?

We are commanded to love God, our friends, and the stranger—but we are *not* commanded to love our parents. We are supposed to *honor* and *fear* our parents (one of the Ten Commandments); honoring and fearing is different from loving. Even the best parent–child relationships may be complicated. This is truer for someone with a disparaging or distant parent. The rabbis teach that if you cannot love your parents, at least respect them. Honor them to the best of your ability, with strong, clear boundaries.[37]

"For love is fierce as death. . . . Its darts are darts of fire, a blazing flame"[38]

We end this chapter with these words from Song of Songs, which teach us that love, in all of its forms, is one of the most powerful emotions in existence, so fierce in its various applications that it is equivalent to the experience of dying. Rabbi Adin Steinsaltz teaches that sometimes feelings of love are so overpowering as to be inescapable.[39] Judaism also understands that it is not always possible to love—not all of your family members, and certainly not all the strangers. Just because you cannot love does not mean that you have to hate.[40]

Chapter 3

The Way of *Simcha*: Happiness + Celebration

I find it fascinating that among all of the promises our Founding Fathers could have made in the Declaration of Independence, they chose not only "life" and "liberty" but also "the pursuit of happiness." Why is the pursuit of happiness the goal, rather than prosperity, entrepreneurship, or fairness? Why are we guaranteed life and liberty, but only the *pursuit* of happiness? Perhaps the founders understood that no individual person can guarantee happiness for anyone else.

Unfortunately, many of us double down on the pursuit. Our culture is built on a happiness insatiability factor. We need more, bigger, faster—and if we get it, we'll be happier. Contemporary expressions of happiness may include feeling firmly grounded in the present, instant gratification, indulging in sugary food and drink, shopping for more stuff (aka "retail therapy"), the dopamine hit of social media. When we get something we want, we think it will make us happy. But we know in our hearts, even as social media posts tell us differently, that no meaningful life can be lived solely as a series of happy moments.

The Jewish definition of the word "happiness" is different from the American one. Judaism understands happiness as bringing pleasure and meaning to others *and also* to you; it's an action that connects you not just to the present moment but to the past and future as well.

Over the millennia, rabbis have given lots of thought to questions such as: How important is it to "be happy"? What is "happiness"? Whose responsibility is my happiness? What is the goal of happiness? What is the goal of laughter and humor? From their many teachings, I have put together the Jewish "commandments" of happiness.

1. True happiness centers the community; the self comes second.

2. Happiness is deeply connected to gratitude.

3. Bringing happiness to others is a spiritual practice.

4. *Shepping nachas* is being happy for other people.

5. Sometimes it's okay to be happy even in the face of sadness.

6. There are lots of different ways to be happy.

7. Living a meaningful life makes you happy.

8. Sometimes you have to force yourself to be happy.

1 True happiness centers the community; the self comes second.

One of the happiest days of my life was July 5, 1998, at the Audubon Society in Maryland. The wedding ceremony—I was the bride—was over. My husband (husband!) and I had spent our first few moments as a married couple together alone and had rejoined the group. Then the hora began.

If you have never been to a hora at a traditional Jewish wedding, let me politely suggest that you find one and crash it. It is wholly (and holy!) chaos. The dancing can go on for an hour and includes exuberant circle dancing, acrobatics, juggling, and other party tricks known as *shtick*. The celebrants are lifted up high in chairs. Just about everyone gets involved, unworried about doing something incorrectly. It is a vortex of unabashed happiness. I was happy.

In trying to dissect why my husband and I were so happy in that moment, it may be easy to come to the conclusion that it was because we were the center of attention, doted upon by 150 of our closest friends and family. When I look back at pictures of the hora, however, the first thing I notice is that I cannot even tell where I *am* in the melee.

I see my friend JJ (z"l; may his memory be for a blessing) juggling for the group. I see the top of my husband's head, as he carries my brother on his shoulders and dances with him high above the crowd on the dance floor. I see my grandmother and my husband's grandmother (z"l) dancing together. I see one hora circle inside another hora circle inside another one, celebrating me and my husband, and the community in which we were raised, and that we had built.

Compare that image to the American-style wedding "first dance," in which the couple performs, all alone, while the guests watch. The Jewish hora centers the community, not the individuals. The couple at this moment is the means to the end, which is *simcha*, or joy.

The joy at my wedding didn't come about because we had a fancy band or were at a fancy hotel. It was July in Maryland. We were in a room with no air conditioning. My father-in-law sweated through three different shirts. It was a happy time because it was about me and my husband, but it also was about so much more—about sharing community and participating in a Jewish act that goes back millennia and will, I hope, be around for millennia to come. It was bigger than either of us.

In Judaism, happiness is not an individual practice. This teaching jibes with contemporary research, which proves that the more connected people feel to a "community" (as they define it), the happier they are.[1] Hedonism, a type of pleasure seeking that centers only the self, is considered ephemeral and pointless. If the pursuit of happiness is primarily or entirely self-indulgent, Judaism holds that it is not meaningful—and can even be dangerous, if it leads to people not caring for the world around them.

A hora of just me and my husband would have been quite pathetic. If the goal of the wedding was, as it is for many weddings, cultivating abundant joy, then we needed to share our happiness rather than hoard it. Our guests needed to find their spark of happiness for us, and share their own.

Happiness shared grows exponentially. Joy comes from being connected to all that is larger than you are in the world, whether that is spirituality or community.[2] It comes from a profound acknowledgment of not-aloneness and connection. The happiness you get is dependent on the joy you help give.

2 Happiness is deeply connected to gratitude.

When the alarm goes off in the morning, and you start to return to consciousness, what thoughts first come to mind? Too often, they are thoughts of what you lack. "I didn't get enough sleep," you think, or "I don't have enough time to get what I want done today." "My job isn't fulfilling," "I want more time to myself," or "I am alone." We may begin each day with a mindset of deprivation and not possibility.

Judaism offers a different orientation. Every morning, before we even get out of bed, we are instructed to offer a few words of gratitude for the one universal thing that all of us who wake up share: sentience. *Modeh Ani*, we say, we are grateful that we have woken up! We're grateful that we are breathing and have the opportunity to try all over again. We begin with gratitude, and the expectation is that it will bring us into joy. The Hebrew term for "gratitude" is *hakarat hatov*, or recognizing the good, acknowledging that there is almost always something for which to be grateful, if only we look for it, search it out, or simply open our eyes in the morning.

The more gratitude we feel and express, the happier we are. In one study, half the participants were asked to spend some time each day making a list of things for which they were grateful. The other half were asked to write about things that annoyed or angered them. After a few weeks, guess which group reported being happier? It wasn't even a contest.[3]

I don't want to oversimplify reality. Given life's fluctuations, expressing gratitude is not always easy. "I lost my job, but at least I'm breathing!" is easier said than believed. Some people are born optimists and some are not. Gratitude comes easier for some than for others.[4] Judaism understands this fact and cultivates an entire discipline around gratitude. Every morning, in addition to the initial Modeh Ani prayer, there are dozens of other prayers that express thanks for everything from the environment to the ability to go to the bathroom, from being free to being able to tell the difference between daytime and nighttime.

Many of these gratitude prayers do double duty: They center us and help us be grateful for what is, and orient us toward all that is possible in the future. I might be free, and for that I am grateful. What does *freedom* mean? How do I express that freedom? Where do I remain metaphorically enslaved? Gratitude is unusual in that it is an end unto itself (take a breath and be grateful; you are alive), and it challenges us to continue learning and growing, and asking Mary Oliver's famous question, "What is it you plan to do with your one wild and precious life?"[5]

3 Bringing happiness to others is a spiritual practice.

There is a story of a man—let's call him Jonah—who wanted to understand the types of people who make it to the World-to-Come, which is a Jewish approximation of heaven. Jonah asked around, and finally a prophet named Elijah told him about two men who were definitely going to get there. Jonah found the men and asked them, "What is your job?" "We are jesters," they said, "and we cheer up those who are sad."[6]

In Judaism, those who help people laugh are the ones who make it to heaven. This task was so important that it became a profession: the *badchan*, who, for many hundreds of years, and still today in certain Jewish communities, is a hired master of ceremonies, comedian, and entertainer who performs at weddings and Jewish holiday celebrations to encourage joy.

Judaism holds that it is imperative to help other people feel joy. In celebratory times such as the Jewish holiday of Sukkot, adults in a household are responsible to make themselves "super-duper happy" (yes, that is a technical term in the Bible), and also their children, anyone who works for them, their local religious leaders, and all those in their neighborhood who are needy.[7] This includes purchasing gifts of material and mundane things like new clothes and sweet treats. One medieval rabbi took this teaching so seriously that he argued that people who hoard happiness for themselves and their families and do not share it with others should be as embarrassed as someone who walks around with feces on their face.[8]

On the Jewish holiday of Purim, we are not supposed to just *be* happy but also to *do* happy. We are required to give friends gifts of sweets (at least two kinds!) so they can more fully enjoy the holiday. We make big celebratory meals and serve each other copious amounts of food and drink. Bringing other people joy is one of the core parts of the holiday experience. It also makes you happier, as well. In one study, participants were given cash-filled envelopes. Those who donated the money to charity or who gave people gifts ended up happier than those who spent the money on themselves. The more money people spent on others, the happier they were.[9] It's a win-win situation. Making other people feel happy makes you feel happy, too.

4 *Shepping nachas* is being happy for other people.

What kind of social media user are you? When scrolling through Instagram, TikTok, or Facebook, do you "like" every post you see? None of them? Have you ever refrained from liking a post because you were jealous of the poster or surprised at how many likes the post already had? Holding back on "liking" even though you know that it would give someone else pleasure and would cost you absolutely nothing except the one-eighth of a second that it takes to press the heart emoji? Maybe it's just me.

I once read that Yiddish, a Jewish language from Eastern Europe, is the only language that has a term for taking pride in other people's accomplishments: shepping nachas. In a world that is often competitive, how lovely to believe that being happy for others and feeling a sense of pride and joy in their accomplishments helps us be happy.

This might feel countercultural in today's binary culture in which people are either "winners" or "losers," without much in between. We valorize a type of competition that comes from a scarcity mindset. Instead, maybe take a lesson from social media—there actually *are* enough "likes" for all of us! We can live in the abundance of unlimited likes and shared happiness.

Shepping nachas is much easier said than done. In the Torah, there are a lot of complicated sibling relationships, but there is one sibling group that truly loves one another, even if they fight from time to time: the triumvirate of Moses, Miriam, and Aaron. We learn that when Aaron finds out that his younger brother, Moses, is being elevated to take over the leadership of the Israelite people, he is "happy in his heart."[10] Because Aaron is able to be happy for his brother, he is rewarded by becoming the high priest of the nation, a job second only to his brother's.[11]

Judaism teaches that happiness breeds more happiness. Being happy for others is both an end in itself and a means to an end. Imagine that your favorite sports team loses the game. You go to work the next day and see a friend whose team won. (In this scenario, the teams were not playing against each other.) Can you find it in yourself to glean a little bit of joy from your friend's happiness? Can it give you a sense of possibility that maybe your team will win again? While you will never be as happy as if your team had won its game, that doesn't mean you have no space for happiness at all. Other people's happiness and accomplishments can buoy us. Happiness is like a candle. You can use it to light another candle without diminishing any of your own light.

Shepping nachas for others cannot be a primary method for gaining a sense of personal joy. We all know parents whose happiness depends on their child's performing in a certain way, which leads to parents who put undue pressure on their children, with the result that no one is happy. Be careful if your desire for shepping nachas tips over into needing to get your happiness from another person.

5 Sometimes it's okay to be happy even in the face of sadness.

Jews have been celebrating Purim for about 2,400 years. On this joyous holiday, celebrated in late February or in March, Jews mark the fact that an evil man named Haman conspired with a silly king named Ahasuerus to kill all the Jews in the kingdom. A brave Jewish queen named Esther partnered with her uncle Mordechai to get the king to overturn his decree. The Jews were saved and their enemies killed. "They tried to kill us, we won, let's eat" became the tongue-in-cheek way to describe the holiday that we have celebrated ever since. We have parties and give each other gifts. We dress in costumes and drink lots of alcohol (only if it is safe). It is one of the happiest days of the year in the Jewish calendar.

Over the course of about three thousand years, Jews have often responded to horror with as much joy as we could harness. We have celebrated baby namings in deportation camps, coming-of-age ceremonies in bomb shelters, and weddings in oncology wards. We privilege joy whenever possible, even in difficult times, "laughing and crying with the same eyes," as a famous poem teaches.[12] We are even taught in the Talmud that if a funeral procession and a wedding procession meet at a crossroads, the wedding—the joyous celebration—should be allowed to proceed first.[13]

Marking a joyous moment in a difficult time is not intended to minimize whatever pain we or others are experiencing. Happiness should be a form of empowerment, not of denial. It can be dangerous to ignore how much suffering remains in the world and in our own lives. Instead, allow the joy to humanize us and remind us that we are all deserving of dignity. Joy is a form of resistance and an expression of gratitude for all that we have and all that we share. People or life's vicissitudes will try to break you; do not let them. Seize joy whenever possible.

We all know people who always feel the need to look at the bright side and smile through the most difficult moments, whose loyalty to feeling (or performing) happiness is an attempt to suffocate anger, sadness, or frustration. Judaism has stop-gap measures to prevent us from falling into this trap. Every one of our prayer services has at least one moment of sadness, as we remember loved ones who have passed away. Even the Jewish wedding, a locus of unambiguous happiness, has a moment of glass-breaking to remind us that brokenness exists in the world. "Rejoice—with trembling!" teaches one core text, a reminder that, while a life entirely given over to sadness is a type of capitulation, a life composed entirely of joy is usually false and its own type of misery.[14]

6 There are lots of different ways to be happy.

Hebrew has at least fifteen words for "joy" or "happiness."

- Simcha: a joyous gathering like a wedding; continuous, internal gladness
- Sasson: external expression of one's internal happiness
- Gila: an exuberant outburst of joy; the happiness of discovery
- Rina: a revitalizing, "refreshing" happiness, often related to singing
- Ditza: sublime joy, often related to dancing

- Tzahala: a cry or shout for joy
- Aliza: exultation or rejoicing
- Chedva: the happiness of togetherness
- Osher: deep happiness, like the kind felt by a great-grandmother surrounded by family
- Alitza: cheer
- Ora: happiness like a light shining brightly upon you and the world around you; uplift
- Teru-ah: a shout of joy; also the longest sound of the shofar, a ram's-horn trumpet used to mark Rosh Hashanah, the Jewish New Year
- Asher: the happiness that comes from abundance
- Nachat: prideful joy
- Ra'anan: being so overcome as to cry or shout with joy[15]

This list reminds us that happiness can manifest itself in many ways and may be defined differently depending on who is experiencing it. For some of us, it will be in large parties, such as celebrating with your community or dancing with the Torah at the Jewish holiday of Simchat Torah. For others, it will be in quiet, celebratory meals with one or two friends. Happiness may look different depending on what stage of life you are in, whether you are more of an introvert or an extrovert, whether you prefer singing, dancing, great conversation, or quiet contemplation. Some people try to learn their loved ones' "love language." It might benefit us to also find our loved ones' "happiness language." And our own as well!

7 Living a meaningful life makes you happy.

Jews pursue happiness with tremendous vigor. Consider the Nazirite, the ancient ascetic who was forbidden to drink alcohol. One might think that God and the religious leadership would be grateful for every Nazirite that joined the order, for they were dedicating themselves to holy services. But we learn that at the conclusion of their time in the Nazirite order, Nazirites had to give a sin offering in the Temple. They had to *atone* for joining God's religious order! It is taught that this is because upon entering the order, the Nazirite would no longer be allowed to drink wine, and God had created wine for us to enjoy safely. We are meant to embrace *all* that God has given us, and be "happy."

Here are Judaism's top ten attributes for a life well lived: justice, grace, humility, repentance, service to God, Torah (Jewish learning), acts of lovingkindness, judgment, truth, and peace. Not found in any of these lists is any one of the fifteen words for happiness listed earlier. What we see over and over again are acts centered on caring for others, not ourselves, ones that are connected not just to the present moment but to all that has come before and all that is yet to come.

Meaningful acts bring "happiness." The more generous a person is, the happier she is.[16] We may think that a week of sunbathing on the beach is going to make us happy, and it might. Try also volunteering regularly at a local shelter. See what makes you feel better, and perhaps you will begin to include in your definition of personal happiness "something we do for others to make ourselves feel better." Happiness is in the service of service.

Whatever inspires you to be happy, whether contemporary science, ancient texts, or personal experience, Judaism wants you to strive for a happy life. But I encourage you to define happiness according to Jewish tradition, which dictates that a happy life is a *meaningful* life.

Marrying my husband was the best decision I ever made. But happiness 24-7? Three kids, two careers, one mortgage. We have something beautiful—and happy—but it's certainly not a hedonic treadmill of unabated joy. Happiness is the result of a life meaningfully lived, which is what we have. It is not happiness that leads to a meaningful life, it is a meaningful life that leads to happiness.

8 Sometimes you have to force yourself to be happy.

Some may argue that one reason Jews have so many holidays centered around finding happiness and are instructed to find happiness even in the most difficult of times is because of our tendency toward pessimism, sadness, and negativity. From the moment we meet the Israelite people in Egypt until the moment the Torah ends, basically all we did was complain. At one point in the desert, "the Israelites wept and said, 'If only we had meat to eat! We remember the fish that we used to eat free in Egypt, the cucumbers, the melons, the leeks, the onions, and the garlic. Now our gullets are shriveled. There is nothing at all! Nothing but this manna to look to!'"[17] While we can all have some compassion for the Israelites' nostalgia, remember that in this instance they are being nostalgic for food they ate while *enslaved*. We see resonances of this attitude in contemporary Jewish humor, which often has the same tone as the Israelites of millennia ago: slightly self-deprecating, ironic, and clever (always clever!). The scholar Dr. Deborah Lipstadt writes that Jewish life is lived on a spectrum: Joy on one end; Oy on the other. ("Oy" is a Yiddish word implying dismay.) Jews find themselves more experienced with the "oy" end. The answer to the classic joke "How many Jewish mothers does it take to change a light bulb" is, "Don't worry about me, I'll just sit here in the dark. Oy."

In the eighteenth century, Rabbi Nachman of Bratslav argued that all people have to do when they are sad is "transform gloom and all suffering into joy." He paints an image of a party, with lots of people happy and dancing, and some people, the sad ones, standing off to the side. Against this person's will, he says, the happy people should bring the sad one into the circle and "force him to be happy along with them." When this happens, he argues, "gladness and joy will catch up with and seize the sadness and sighing," and the person will be happy.[18]

Really, all someone has to do to become happy is to join the circle? After being *forced* to do so?

As a rabbi, I have spent time with many people who are in the throes of depression or general brokenheartedness. "Introducing them, against their will, into joy" does not work. This is true anecdotally, and research proves it. You cannot force someone into happiness.[19] Even the old saw that smiling makes you happier is not entirely true. Forcing yourself to smile does increase dopamine levels, making you feel "happier." Those "happy" feelings are fleeting, however, and the letdown after the dopamine level drops can make you feel even worse.[20]

On the other hand, research proves that you *can* train yourself to be optimistic, and that optimism leads to happiness. Imagining your ideal future can increase optimism[21] because it helps you think "about all your dreams coming true as opposed to worrying about the worst possible outcome."[22] In the words of Laura Oliff, a cognitive therapist, consider the "very valuable" and "joyful" feelings of "positive anticipation." There are moments in which we can choose to think about what we are anticipating with joy or with dread. If there is a choice, why not choose the more positive option? The only person who can "force" you into optimism is you. While it is not guaranteed, there is a chance that more optimism will bring more happiness.

I now choose to understand Rabbi Nachman differently. Other people can *encourage* happiness by reinforcing optimistic stances, gently and lovingly inviting you into "the circle." Only you have the power to take them up on their offer.

For those who are suffering from clinical depression or other illnesses that keep happiness walled off, the amount of work it takes to enter "the circle" can be overwhelming, making the circle inaccessible. In those moments, I hope you can sense that you are not alone, that there are others willing to accompany you until you can enter the circle again.

Chapter 4

The Way of *Guf*: The Body

There's a rabbinic story about a rabbi named Elazar. He was traveling home on his donkey, happy with himself because he had spent the day studying with his favorite teacher. He was filled with self-confidence, and as he rode along, he thought of himself as great and smart. All of a sudden, Elazar noticed a man. We'll call him Joe.

Joe: "Peace be upon you, sir."

Elazar (surprised): "Whoa. You are quite ugly! Is everyone in your town as ugly as you?"

Joe (unperturbed): "I actually don't know! Do me a favor: Find the Artist who made me, and tell the Craftsman that I'm an ugly vessel."

At that moment, Elazar realized he had been a thoughtless jerk. Who had made Joe but the very same Artist that Elazar served, the very same God who, Elazar was taught, created every single human being in God's image—including Joe?

Elazar got down from his donkey and bowed low before Joe, begging forgiveness. Joe was not having it.

Joe said, "Go find the Artist and say to the Artist, 'How ugly is the vessel which you have made.'"

Joe continued walking, with Elazar close behind, begging.

As Joe and Elazar came into town, the citizens came out to meet Elazar, calling out in excitement that someone they considered to be one of their most thoughtful teachers had returned to them. Joe became confused, because of course he only knew Elazar as the person who had humiliated him.

Joe said to the townspeople, "Who is the teacher that you are celebrating?"

"That's Rabbi Elazar behind you," the townspeople replied.

Joe (rolling his eyes), "If *he's* what you would consider to be a good teacher, then I truly hope that there are no more teachers at all among the Jews." He then told the stunned townspeople what Elazar had said to him.

They responded, "That *is* terrible. Maybe you should forgive him, because he is a learned teacher."

Joe replied, "Fine. On one condition. He may never again critique another body. We are each created in God's image."

The people agreed. Our tradition teaches that they all lived happily, and gently, ever after.[1]

In Judaism, bodies, with their diversity of size, shape, color, and ability, are not meant to be critiqued but to be celebrated. Our job is to take care of them. Our bodies help us realize our values and bring more goodness into the world.[2] Each of our bodies is created in the divine image.

About ten years ago, I led a trip to Israel for a synagogue group that included many people who had recently converted to Judaism. One of those participants, Janet, described herself as a "proper girl from the South." She had grown up in a strictly Christian family; her parents were so religious that she had not yet found the strength to tell them that she had converted to Judaism. When she told them about the trip to Israel, for instance, she did not specify that it was a *Jewish* trip.

One very hot day, the group hiked through a dry ravine in the southern Negev desert. It was an out-and-back hike, two hours in each direction. We encouraged participants to drink copious amounts of water, and they listened. When we were about halfway through the hike, Janet walked up to me and demurely asked where the "facilities" were.

"Everywhere you look," I said playfully, indicating the stark landscape around us. Translation: There were no bathrooms. If someone needed to go, they would have to squat behind a bush.

Janet blushed. "I'll wait until we get back to the bus," she said.

We continued walking. An hour later we were still far from the bus and Janet came over to me, slightly hunched over. "Okay, you win, Rabbi," she said as if it was I who was somehow hiding the facilities. "I will go behind that bush."

We let the rest of the group walk ahead and I stood guard, my back turned to give her privacy. She delicately walked over to the bush and relieved herself. When she returned, she looked me square in the eye and said, "Rabbi, one day I might be able to tell my parents that I became Jewish. I will *never* be able to admit that I peed behind a bush. We do not talk about such things in my family." We walked on.

In Judaism, celebrating the body means talking about it. We are permitted, encouraged, and sometimes even required to know our bodies well and to take care of our physical needs. Janet and I discussed this fact as we hiked. I taught her about the blessing that we say after using the bathroom, in which we give thanks for our bodies having been formed with "many openings and many hollow spaces. It is obvious and known . . . that if even one of them would be opened, or if even one of them would be sealed, it would be impossible to survive and to stand before You even for one hour." She giggled, embarrassed, and also realized that it's true; without working orifices, we are doomed.

I have not seen Janet in many years, but I hope that she was able to tell her parents both secrets, that of becoming Jewish, and of peeing in the desert. They are not as different from each other as you might think. In one of our sacred texts, the Mishneh Torah, Maimonides argues that "a person should never put off relieving themself, even for an instant. Rather, whenever they need to urinate or move their bowels, they should do so immediately."[3] I include this quote verbatim as an indicator of what is considered sacred in Judaism: not only philosophical navel-gazing about what it means to be created in the divine image but also practical instructions about finding the nearest restroom, even if it is a bush in the desert.

We also have a law that tells you what to do if you are saying your morning prayers and need to pass gas. (Answer: Do them one at a time.[4]) Large portions of the Bible cover diseases of the body, including rashes, oozing pus, and emissions of all sorts. Different bodies are beautiful in different ways; every body is part of creation.

The body as a spiritual tool

In Judaism, our bodies are not only containers for our souls but also active tools for building a meaningful life. Body and soul are interdependent. Think about the differences between talking about building a house, witnessing someone building a house, and building one with our own hands. While we can learn something about home building from each, it is far more meaningful and educational to build with our own hands, and especially to build our own home with our own hands, rather than just talk to someone else about doing it. We use our bodies to understand and build the world around us.

We understand today the concept of different learning modalities. Some people learn best by reading, some by listening, some by doing. Jewish teaching intuitively understands the need for all the different modalities and has a "the whole is greater than the sum of its parts" attitude to learning. When our intellectual, physical, and spiritual faculties experience something in tandem, they can assimilate it more profoundly than if each faculty works alone.

Jewish ritual makes use of embodied practices to help us integrate the meaning of the moment. On Passover we eat the unleavened cracker called *matzah*, embodying the actions of our ancestors who were forced to leave Egypt in a hurry as they escaped slavery.

During the holiday of Sukkot, we live in huts for seven days, just like the agricultural huts that Jews lived in thousands of years ago, when we were farmers in the land of Israel. At the end of Shabbat every week, there is a ceremony called *havdalah* in which we use all our senses to mark the transition from the peaceful moments of Shabbat to the hubbub of the rest of the week. We chant prayers, look at a candle's flame, smell spices, and drink wine.

Our prayer services include choreography that encourages us to remember that our spiritual selves and our physical selves are not separate. The Hebrew word *baruch*, which begins all of our blessings and is often translated as "blessed," comes from the word that means "knee." Baruch is a physical cue that the process of being blessed and of blessing holds within it a sense of humility, a bending of the knee. The funny-sounding Yiddish word *shuckling* is the rhythmic back-and-forth or side-to-side motion that some Jews make while they are praying. Shuckling, like many other repetitive, self-soothing practices, helps worshippers calm and center themselves and better concentrate on what they are saying/praying.

American fast-food culture can sometimes encourage us to experience the body as a passive receptacle and not as a powerful tool for change. But even restrictive embodied practices like fasting, which Jews do a number of times a year, force us to recognize that our bodies are primary parts of our spiritual experience.

How do I keep my body healthy?

There's another rabbinic story about two rabbis, Yishmael and Akiva, who were walking down the street when a sick man found them. Let's call this man Will.

Will said to the rabbis, "My teachers, tell me how I can be healed."

Yishmael and Akiva replied, "Do such-and-such until you are healed."

Will: "How did I get sick?"

Yishmael and Akiva: "God."

Will: "But if God caused my illness, how can you, mere humans, tell me how to heal it? Wouldn't that be transgressing God's will?"

Yishmael and Akiva: "What is your occupation?"

Will: "I am a farmer."

Yishmael and Akiva: "Who created the land you farm?"

Will: "God."

Yishmael and Akiva: "If God created it, how dare you care for it?"

Will (sputtering): "If I did not go out and plow it, fertilize it, weed it, nothing would grow!"

Yishmael and Akiva: "Just as a tree will not grow if it is not weeded, fertilized, and plowed, so, too, with the body. The fertilizer is the medicine and the varieties of healing, and the farmer is the doctor."[5]

I think of this story every time someone tells me that they "believe in science, not religion," as if the two are mutually exclusive. (For those who know the Bible and have questions for me such as, "How can you believe that religion and science are compatible when you read the biblical book of Genesis," I will answer that I stand in a proud line of thousands of years of rabbis who believe that the

Bible should be taken *seriously*, but not *literally*.) In Judaism, "belief in science, not religion" literally does not make sense. Jews who believe in God understand that God created a world with doctors, medicine, and science for us to use them to care for ourselves and our bodies.

Some of you might believe in a God who causes illness; I do not. I believe in a God who has placed a soul in each of our bodies. But how we make use of these bodies, how we keep them healthy or abuse them, is up to us. I believe in a God who has created a world in which we can lessen the possibility of getting sick by eating well, exercising, and getting a lot of sleep. We lessen—but of course never eradicate—the possibility of illness when we take care of both our bodies and our souls.

Pikuach nefesh is a Hebrew term that literally means "guarding the soul," which is more informally translated as "saving a life." Our tradition teaches that we must save a life at almost any cost. This is true whether we are talking about another human being's body or about our own, and it is another reason that caring for our bodies is so critical in Judaism.

Maimonides, who was both a rabbi and a doctor, offers a clear explanation for why we should be concerned with our bodily health and well-being. He argues (and many of us know this from personal experience) that it is near-impossible to fully partake of the world when we are sick. Maimonides teaches that we have to cultivate what he calls "healthful habits" and refrain from harming our bodies as much as we can. His instructions, written almost a thousand years ago, resonate with many of us who attempt to live a healthy lifestyle. Exercise regularly, he says, and bathe afterward. After you exercise, eat good, healthy food, but do not overstuff yourself.[6]

We may not want to follow all of Maimonides's teachings on health. While sleeping eight hours a night, as he recommends, may still be advisable, always eating while reclining on one's left side is not. Science has evolved since the twelfth century; the goal is not to follow his words verbatim. It is to recognize that learning about and practicing the healthy behaviors of our time, as Maimonides surely did in his, is a spiritual practice.

While it is a Jewish duty to visit and heed your doctor,[7] and for physicians to be licensed and work as hard as they can to heal their patients,[8] doctors do not have unequivocal power. The doctor's power only applies when it is *more* protective of the patient than the patient wishes to be. When a doctor would permit something potentially risky but the patient is concerned about an ensuing harm, the Talmud teaches that "the heart knows the bitterness of its own soul" better than any doctor. A human being can understand the extent of being in pain better than any doctor observing that person. An example of this principle is what to do on a major Jewish fast day when Jews traditionally neither eat nor drink for twenty-five hours. If a doctor says that a person should be eligible to fast, but the person does not feel healthy enough to fast, then that person does not fast.[9]

When it comes to vaccinations, the Jewish concept of communal responsibility and pikuach nefesh takes precedence. According to Jewish philosophy, vaccinations are required in almost all instances, and especially when there is a risk of death to even a small proportion of other people who might contract the disease.[10] Vaccinations are required not only for the health of the person receiving it but also—and perhaps even more so—for the sake of the community and to promote herd immunity.[11] People who do *not* get themselves and their children vaccinated are called "thieves" and are censured.[12]

Food and eating

In Judaism, we believe that the food we choose to eat also helps keep our bodies healthy. Judaism has a sacred eating practice called "kashrut," (or "keeping kosher") that goes back thousands of years. Observant Jews do not eat pork or shellfish. They only eat certain birds and only fish with fins and scales. They do not eat "meat" (poultry, beef, and other animals with split hooves and who chew their cud) at the same time as "milk" (any sort of dairy). The laws continue in great detail and have been expanded upon over many centuries.

We don't know the original intent behind the laws of kashrut; we can only give our best guess. Perhaps these laws were an ancient attempt to encourage people to eat more healthily. We are instructed not to eat animals that are ill, for instance, which may seem obvious in the twenty-first century but was not in the second century, a time in which meat was less plentiful and not eating from a sick animal may have meant going without eating at all.

Some argue that Jews keep kosher to learn discipline, and that we are not meant to understand the reasons behind the traditions. Others argue that kashrut was intended to help build a sense of Jewish community. Jews who keep strictly kosher tend to need to eat around other people who eat the same way, which in turn keeps the community more tight-knit, even insular.

For those of us who do not follow the traditional laws of kashrut, there is still much to learn.

Even if we *can* eat something, it doesn't mean that we always *should*. Some things called "food" are not actually healthy for human consumption. Research has shown that ultra-processed foods are unhealthy and should be avoided.[13] Eating too late at night can cause heartburn or acid reflux.[14] Those who are lactose-intolerant, suffer from celiac disease, or have allergies already know that some foods can be dangerous, but for the rest of us, the discipline of not eating everything we lay our eyes on forces us to be more thoughtful about what we do eat and when. Even if you don't want to eat as a traditional observer of kashrut would, you can still make thoughtful choices about what you do eat.

Tradition also teaches that good conversation, not unfettered and unfocused eating, should be the ideal focal point of meals. A rabbi named Shimon taught that at every meal involving three or more people there should be learned and spiritual conversation. Just stuffing our faces with food is a type of idolatry. If three or more people have thoughtful conversations, it makes the meal a meaningful gathering.[15] Someone who eats too casually in the street is disqualified as a witness in a court case because how can you trust a person who does not sit down and appreciate their food?[16] Food fuels human relationships as well as our bodies.

Food is not just fuel; it is also delicious! This belief is evidenced by rabbinic teachings that indicate that we are judged by the pleasurable things we could have eaten but chose not to.[17] In the Bible, we are taught that the Israelites ate manna while they wandered in the desert for forty years after being freed from slavery in Egypt. The Israelites were instructed to take as much manna as they desired, and tradition teaches that the manna tasted like each person's favorite food. The ancient Israelites were invited to eat intuitively, as much as and whenever they wanted.

When we fall ill

There is no Jewish tradition that encourages the ill to passively await healing, without any work on their part. We are expected to seek out doctors, medicine, and other forms of healing.

We are also encouraged to pray, which Judaism believes can have an impact, even for nonbelievers. If ever there is a time at which even an atheist can pray to God, it is when their life or the life of a loved one is endangered.

We don't know if prayer by itself can help someone heal; maybe we'll never know that. Prayer *can*, however, give us a sense of agency in moments of powerlessness. Prayer can allow us to direct complicated emotions, such as anger, sadness, exhaustion, or even wrath in the correct direction: at the universe. Prayer can thus prevent us from directing these feelings in an unhelpful direction, such as toward a friend or family member who has nothing to do with the situation. Prayer can give us hope in even the most difficult moments. Scientists argue that hope is critical and appropriate at all times as long as the person who is hoping (in our case, praying) understands the reality about how likely it is that the hope will be fulfilled.[18] Prayer can remind you that you are not alone, that there are others in what Susan Sontag called "the kingdom of the sick."

Prayer is sometimes considered "successful" even if the person for whom you are praying is not restored to full health. In the Jewish understanding, sometimes the "healing" happens when the person dies and the soul is free. Unlike the majority of Jewish liturgy, which is fixed and has been for hundreds—if not thousands—of years, the healing prayer is more fluid, open to individual needs and interpretations. There is no one right way to do it.

While the specific words of the healing prayer are not universal, the general sentiment of the prayer is. We invoke the memory of our ancestors, on whose shoulders we stand. We ask for "blessing" and "healing" for this specific person. We ask that this person experience God's compassion, and strengthen them, so that they experience a "complete healing" of body and soul, along with all those who are ill. We ask for the healing to come soon. And we end with a rousing "amen," a Hebrew word which means "I agree." When someone in our community is in pain, or when a loved one is ill, we all agree: We hope they are healed.

If prayer can provide unexpected solace when one is ill, so, too, can the presence of one's community. Consider the legend of a rabbi named Hiyya, who became sick. Hiyya's teacher Yochanan came to visit him and asked, "Is your suffering dear to you? Do you want to be sick?"

Hiyya replied, "Absolutely not."

Yohanan then said, "Give me your hand."

Hiyya gave him his hand.

Yochanan grabbed it, and with their hands clasped, Hiyya was healed.

New scene: Yochanan became sick. Another rabbi, Hanina, came to visit him.

Hanina asked, "Is your suffering dear to you? Do you want to be sick?"

Yochanan replied, "Absolutely not."

Hanina then said, "Give me your hand."

Yochanan gave Hanina his hand. Hanina grabbed it, and with their hands clasped, Yochanan was healed.

In telling this story, the rabbis teach that "a prisoner cannot free himself from prison,"[19] which can be read both literally and metaphorically. When we are trapped, when we are suffering, we need to be able to depend on others to remind us of a different, healed future. That we absolutely cannot face illness alone is a starkly different message than one we receive in modern individualistic culture, in which people can feel quite alone—and can be left too alone—in their healing journey. In contrast, there is a Jewish teaching that every person who visits you when you are sick takes away one sixtieth of your illness. Think of the implication of that teaching. It is a great chesed to visit someone who is ill, and we should want to receive a visitor. You, who may be perfectly healthy, should somehow take on the burden of someone else's illness. For the math geeks out there who are thinking to themselves, "Why not just have sixty people visit you and then you'll be healed?" the rabbis have an answer: Every visitor takes away one sixtieth of whatever illness is left from the previous visitor, which means that the number will never reach zero. That also means that the first person to visit takes away more of the illness than anyone else. So be first in line!

We are all interconnected. The tradition of *bikur cholim* (visiting the sick) is considered such a chesed that one who does it receives unlimited spiritual reward. Bikur cholim benefits not only the person who is ill but also the one doing the visiting. In certain situations, visiting an ill person is good for the physical health of the visitor because it makes their immune system stronger.[20] When people visit each other, so-called "mirror neurons" enable emotions to spread from one person to another. People can "infect" each other not only with germs but with moods, including optimism, hope, and possibility.[21] Mirror neurons, by changing one's frame of mind, can be exactly what the "prisoner" needs to be released from their illness. They heal faster.

No matter how much effort we put into healing ourselves, there are moments in which we will need to lean on others. When we do, we can "free ourselves from prison," even in small ways.

Mental health

When I was twenty-four, I worked as director of a Sunday school. I was in charge of the religious education of dozens of young people from kindergarten to high school. I was lucky to be under the supervision of Rabbi Pamela Frydman Baugh, who gently reprimanded me one day when I came to complain to her about a teenage student named Josh.

"He's a sloth," I said. "I ask him a question, and he barely grunts an answer. He moves slowly, isn't kind to other kids in the class, and is so morose that it affects the entire mood of the class, even though he doesn't say anything. I'd like to call his parents and tell them that his behavior needs to change."

Rabbi Pam looked at me, clear-eyed, and said, "Have you not seen that Josh is depressed?"

I had not. She went on to tell me more about his life and about how depression manifests itself in people and especially in teens. I still ended up calling Josh's parents, but with an entirely different affect and agenda than if I had not been brought up short by Rabbi Pam. Instead of making demands, I expressed curiosity, first with the parents, then with Josh, about how best to be of service to Josh in this difficult time. In retrospect, I realize that I was lucky that he was in a place where both he and his parents recognized his depression. Knowing that you are struggling with mental illness is the first step, and often one of the most difficult ones.

A recent study concluded that half of all people on Earth will develop a mental health disorder in their lifetime.[22] The impact that depression and anxiety has on the global economy could be measured in one trillion dollars in lost productivity.[23] These statistics—and our own personal, lived experiences—lay bare what we may already know: Mental health struggles are real, and they are everywhere. It's a good sign that the percentage of adults receiving mental health treatment continues to rise. We are lucky to live in a time in which stigma is on the decline, but there is still a long way to go.

While Judaism gives equal weight to the importance of mental and physical health, we have not always been able to agree on what to do when we need support with our mental health. One fourth-century rabbi says that a person's anxieties should be "forcefully pushed out of his mind," while another argues that they should be "told to everyone." These can be read as different approaches to mental illness or distress, the first one focusing on coping mechanisms and the second on talking it out, which are two of the many schools of mental health care today. However we read these rabbinic statements, it's clear that the rabbis understood that mental health issues do not just disappear. We have to address them.[24]

Today, much of Jewish culture is relatively accepting of psychotherapy. A few studies have proved that Jews, as a group, have greater confidence in therapy, feel less of a stigma around the process, and are more open to sharing their feelings than members of other ethnic or racial groups.[25] It makes sense that Jews are attracted to therapy because Jewish tradition is premised on looking inward and on doing better in the world (*cheshbon hanefesh* in Hebrew). Jews are exposed to this mindset from a very young age.

Many rabbis over the course of history have shared their wisdom on mental health. The seventeenth-century teacher Rabbi Nachman is thought to have been depressed himself and wrote a lot about sadness and joy. In Nachman's opinion, being bitter or sad is human nature. Everyone is full of troubles. In spite of that, he argued, people should try with all their might to always be happy.

If we must, we can set aside up to an hour a day for brokenhearted-ness, he said. The rest of the time, we should be happy.[26]

   Rabbi Nachman does not tell us to have "good vibes only." He figures out what to do, given what he calls an "existential condi-tion of lack." As with Maimonides's medical advice earlier in this chapter, I offer his teachings here not because I think they should be taken literally but because they should be taken seriously. When "must" we be happy? When do we accept sadness as "a condition of being human?" What can we learn from scholars who are study-ing these topics that we can apply to our own lives?

   With mental illness, as with physical illness, tradition teaches that caring for yourself is critical. The biblical King Saul had an "evil spirit" that "terrified" him. His advisers gave him advice: The lyre was known to help people feel better when they were overcome by evil spirits. King Saul asked his advisers to find someone who could play well. They found a young shepherd named David, who came to play the lyre before the king, and this made the king feel better for a time.[27]

   In King Saul's story, people who were watching out for the king's well-being noticed when his mood shifted. This, too, is another rea-son for the importance of community when thinking about car-ing for the body. We might not notice changes in ourselves because they come upon us gradually, or we think they are typical of other human beings or are just part of "normal" aging. Sometimes we do notice but are too embarrassed or ashamed to say anything. Sometimes someone else needs to begin the conversation.

   When the king was offered a solution, he agreed to try it. This is not always the case. Sometimes people don't recognize that they need help, so suggesting solutions just aggravates them. In addition, mental health care is both expensive and difficult to access. Agreeing to the lyre player, the therapist, or the medication can be much more complicated than the Bible makes it seem. In moments of clarity, when you see the world well enough to know that something is off in your brain or in that of a loved one and that neither of you deserves the pain, I hope the king's story encourages you to reach out and try to find solutions or methods that lead the way to healing.

Chronic pain

It is estimated that more than almost 20 percent of the world's population (about 1.5 billion people) are afflicted with some sort of chronic pain.[28]

For those of us who do not live with chronic pain, it can be difficult to have compassion for those who do, especially for those with "low-impact" pain. *Have you tried this cure?* We ask. Or: *Just don't think about it. Are you sure it's not psychosomatic?* I sympathize with the feelings of impotence associated with bearing witness to a loved one's pain, yet sentiments like "Just walk it off" do nothing to help the sufferer, and can harm them even further. Glib remarks or flippant advice minimize another's pain, suggesting that we can fully understand their experience when we cannot. A comment such as, "Can't you just get over it?" even when made without malice, is not only insensitive but also can be interpreted as, "Here's what I need you to do for me," which centers the needs of the healthy person instead of the one in pain. A more helpful question to ask is, "What can I do for you?"

It is understandable if someone living with chronic pain loses hope that they will recover. And it *is* true that in the Jewish tradition, holding false hope is forbidden. One cannot pray for something that has already happened, for instance. If you're pregnant, you're not allowed to pray you will have a girl or a boy, because the sex of the baby has already been determined. That is called a "prayer in vain."[29] Our sages teach that anyone who prays and prays and expects a different answer will ultimately come to heartache.[30] We also learn that we are forbidden to rely on miracles.[31]

On the other hand, Jews have always quipped that "we do not have the luxury of despair." Abandoning hope altogether is also forbidden. What to do, then, in cases of chronic illness or pain?

In what you may see at first as a non sequitur, I want to share the story of a sex worker named Rahab. It's a few thousand years ago, as the Israelites are poised to enter the land of Canaan after being freed from slavery in Egypt. Joshua, who has taken over as leader after Moses's death, sends out two scouts, telling them, "Go, look over the land, especially Jericho." Apparently, the men thought that "Go, look over the land" meant "Go find a sex worker," so the men went directly to Rahab's home, the text teaches, "and stayed there."[32]

The Canaanites hear that there are Israelites at Rahab's home. Soldiers knock on Rahab's door to slaughter the Israelites, but she thinks fast, hiding the scouts and telling the soldiers that there are no Israelites in her home. The soldiers leave. In gratitude, the scouts promise that when the Israelite army invades Canaan, they will not touch Rahab or anyone in her family. All she has to do is tie a cord (*tikvah*) of scarlet thread outside the window so the Israelites will know who she is. She and her family are saved.

That Hebrew word "tikvah" is a homonym, meaning both "cord" and "hope." This gives me solace. According to Jewish tradition, hope is not meant to be a tidal wave. Instead, we find hope in a thin red thread, which people from a number of faith traditions wear today to ward off the evil eye or to symbolize good luck. Sometimes, we need to hold on to the thinnest of threads.

In Judaism, hope is an attitude, not a strategy. What saved Rahab and her family was not just sitting back and waiting for God to provide. It was the courage to have hope in the midst of fear or uncertainty, anger or apathy. When we find ourselves in difficult situations, we can consciously decide that no matter what happens, we are not going to wait for the end but build a new future, even one that is very different from what we imagined.

In Judaism, many verbs are not ends unto themselves; they require further action. The word *zachor*, for instance, means not just "remember" but "remember so that." Tikvah can mean not just "hope" but "hope—and then do." The Talmud teaches that we are not permitted to rely on a miracle.[33] Hope requires ongoing action, even if it's only a thread's worth.

Chapter 5

The Way of *Mamon*: Money

Historically, insidious stereotypes about Jews and money have been used to disparage, oppress, and murder Jews. Even the Hebrew word *mamon*, meaning "money," became a negative term. Jews have been accused of being both stingy and extravagant, money-hoarding and profligate, in control of the world's banks, and dangerous communists determined to overturn capitalism and steal the boss's hard-earned money. It should go without saying that while there *are* individual Jews (just as there are non-Jews) in each of the above categories, none of the above is true for all Jews or even for a majority of Jews.

In this chapter, we will change the conversation. We'll move away from stereotypes, misnomers, and outright lies, diving instead into values and aspirations embedded within Judaism. I am proud of how Jews understand our responsibilities around money, both how we earn it and how we spend it.

Money as a driving force

When my husband and I first started planning how to simultaneously help pay for our kids' college educations and save for our retirement, it became immediately clear that financial planning is as much about exploring our values as about maxing out our IRAs. Questions we considered include: Is there an amount of money that we could save after which we would feel comfortable retiring? Should our children get an inheritance when we die, or should we leave it all to charity? What type of spending is too extravagant? We revisit these conversations regularly, as our circumstances and worldview evolve.

Money is a driving force in the world. If we do not have enough of it, we will not have food on the table or shelter over our heads. If we have too much, we are complicit in an economy in which the richest one percent own almost 50 percent of the world's wealth, while the poorest half of the world owns 0.75 percent. A world in which, since 2020, for every dollar of new wealth gained by someone in the bottom 90 percent, one of the world's billionaires has gained $1.7 million.[1]

How do you feel as you read those statistics? Are you incensed because of the wealth disparity? Or apathetic because you feel powerless to do anything about it? Did you assume that whoever is rich deserves their money because they work harder than everyone else? Or did you look at the statistics about the rich and the poor and think to yourself, "I am neither rich nor poor, so I am not part of the problem"?

Judaism challenges us to continually ask questions and to always see ourselves as part of both the problem and the solution. If spent thoughtfully and generously, money can be a critical tool used to transform the world, building a life of meaning and equality for ourselves, our families, our community, and all of humanity. If hoarded or spent only for one's own good, money can destroy a society. And while the rich have a tremendous amount of power, that does not mean that the poor have none. Every human being, if we work together, can help bring about positive change.

Before we begin with Judaism, let's start with *you*. What money messages did you receive from your family of origin or the culture around you? Think about your parents, grandparents, role models, or anyone who has ever influenced you, the television shows or movies you watched, the magazines you read, the websites you perused. What have they taught you, implicitly or explicitly? "You don't have enough," "Time is money," "Live within your means," "Give what you can, whenever you can," "Save for a rainy day," "Your elders sacrificed for you," "Do whatever you can to make an extra dollar."[2] Consider the values that you want to keep and develop and those you want to let go. Have conversations with friends and family about them. Keep yourself open—over the course of a lifetime—to the possibility of discerning new messages and sloughing off others.

Judaism has a few core teachings about money.

1. We are stewards of our money; it does not belong to us.

2. Every penny made and every penny spent is a reflection of our values.

3. Acquiring wealth is acceptable as long as the money is used to do more good and less harm to the world and its inhabitants.[3]

4. Being poor is a burden. Asceticism is not a virtue.

5. Straightforward and thoughtful conversations about money have the potential to build stronger communal structures.

6. Money can motivate us to do more good in the world.

Who does our money belong to?

When my children were little, they would each get thirty minutes a day to use the family iPad. They were permitted to go to any kid-friendly website they wanted and play games, watch TV, or even window-shop. When their time was up, no matter how I approached the child, often they would desperately hold on to the iPad, yelling "Mine!" I would explain that, even though they still had *physical* control of the iPad, it was not theirs. It was the family's, and it was now their sibling's turn.

You are likely not surprised that this "Mine!" impulse is not just reserved for children; it is often even worse among adults. We argue that whatever we have is "ours," and refuse to share. We give many justifications for what it is that we hold on to so tightly, "I deserve it" being the most popular explanation. In those grasping moments we often don't think of the advantages that helped us to gain what we are holding so tightly—that we received a free education, perhaps, or that a friend helped us get a first job, or that our type of intelligence is more valued than other types and therefore remunerated at a higher salary level. Even when we do decide to share what we have, we may expect others to feel *lucky* to receive whatever we decide to give.

When it comes to money, Judaism holds that humans are like my children, the iPad is our money, and the family is God. Our money does not belong to us but to God. We are the stewards of what we have earned or inherited[4] and are responsible and accountable for how we use the money in our possession.[5] This is a stunning, transformative concept, and paradoxical. On the one hand, we are being asked to loosen the grip on "our" money by sharing more. On the other hand, we are supposed to be thoughtful before we spend our money, making sure we do not waste it, for we all have to answer for our financial decisions.

Believing that the money belongs to God requires a sense of humility; what we think of as "ours" is not. This belief helps those with less money not to feel inferior to those with more and is supposed to help those with more money not to feel superior to those with less. The amount of money we have or make has a lot to do with our actions but is not entirely dependent on it.

"Every person for themself" is a profoundly un-Jewish statement. Replacing it with a stewardship model can help you build an approach to making, saving, and spending money that shifts your perspective from a "taking" mentality to one of "partnership," between you and the universe, or you and humanity.

Is money "good" or "bad"?

Some might argue that money is the root of all evil; Judaism does not. Money is to a certain extent value neutral. If used to make the world a more fair or loving place, or to help you and your community enjoy life a little bit more, it's very good!

The urge to accumulate an egregious amount of money, however, is viewed negatively. Often, that urge comes from coveting that which your neighbor or colleague has. Aggressive competitiveness at best leads people to spend too much time focused on making money, and at worst is exploitative of the Earth and of other humans.[6] According to our prophetic tradition, there is no instance in which making money is more important than making the world a more "godly" place.[7]

We may think we can accumulate tremendous wealth without it affecting our character, but this is often untrue. King Solomon himself—who was famously very wise—thought he could accumulate wealth and wives without falling into sin. (We know better than to think of partners as assets in this way.) Spoiler alert: Even wise King Solomon found his best judgment swayed by the lure of money.[8]

A sense of determination to make some money is critical to building a good life. The impulse to make money can be compared to the impulse to have sex. They are both good things, but too much of them, or doing them in a way that is harmful to others, is dangerous.[9] While money is a driving force in the world, the drive to acquire it should not rule over you.

As a way to de-emphasize the importance of money in society and for each of us as individuals, the Bible offers us the traditions of *shmita* and *yovel*. Every seventh year, both in ancient times and today in Israel, farmers let their land lie fallow for an entire year. As they allow the land to rejuvenate itself, they lose much of their income for that year. And every fifty years, in yovel, or jubilee year, the land reverts back to its "original owner." While it is not clear whether yovel was ever practiced, ancient and contemporary rabbis teach that the goal of yovel was to deconcentrate wealth and put into practice the idea that what we have is not ours. There was no such thing as "private property" as the term is currently understood. To a certain extent, we, in partnership with God, have equal shares in production.

What is the right way to acquire wealth?

In Judaism, we are commanded to work.[10] We understand engaging in work as part of the covenant established at creation: There is no reward without responsibility.[11] In the first chapters of the Bible, God creates a world in which humans are given dominion over the Earth, but only if they do the labor of cultivating it.[12] The famous anti-war statement from the biblical book of Isaiah teaches that we will know when peace has come because we will beat our swords into plowshares, providing not a complete rest but rather the means to work the land.[13]

Whatever we do for a living, we are taught that work should help build a more sacred and holy world. *Avodah*, one of the Hebrew words for "work," also means "divine service." Whether our work is white- or blue-collar, whether it requires a university education or not, it should support human flourishing and not denigrate the Earth or others. Many of the most influential rabbis in Jewish history were employed as woodchoppers, builders, field laborers, gravediggers, cotton dealers, cattle farmers, and beer brewers.[14] Work keeps people involved in society and connected one to the other; at its best, it promotes diversity across all kinds of difference.

Judaism doesn't believe that wealth comes only from luck, or from some secret that only a few know, or because the Jews are "God's Chosen Ones." Jews believe that financial success comes from working hard and teaching our children to do so—as well as from privilege and a lucky break here and there. We value those who work the land and those who spend long days building businesses. Work keeps people away from missteps of all sorts because it occupies the mind, helps people save money for an uncertain future, allows us to express our free will, and provides a sense of dignity. Working is a Jewish value.[15]

No matter how rich you are, Judaism teaches that not working is not optimal. The ancient rabbis worried that money that comes too easily, or without working, might cause a person to make harmful choices. One rabbinic story tells of a wealthy man who gave his son large amounts of money and then took him to the entrance of a brothel. Ancient rabbis deemed the gift unseemly, and blamed the father, arguing that the son had so much money that he had almost no choice but to spend it in unsavory ways. While our tradition encourages people to take responsibility for their own actions, the rabbis' point here is clear. Too much money coupled with too little responsibility can lead people in the wrong direction.[16]

"Work" does not only mean paid labor. We are instructed not to be idle as much as we are instructed to work. Judaism recognizes the unpaid labor of those who take care of their home or children, or who work by volunteering in the community. The "work" of Torah study is also valued. Our time is supposed to be filled with activity for good.[17]

While work is critical, overwork is unacceptable. This is why we have Shabbat and other forms of ceasing from everyday activities. Working too hard makes you less wise, not more, because it doesn't permit you to diversify your learning or life experiences.[18]

How much money is "enough"?

One reason it is difficult to know how much money is "enough" is because it's entirely relative. There is no absolute or objective amount that denotes "enough." For some, "wealthy" is having $2.2 million in assets. For others, it's having just enough to live on, plus an ample amount of free time.[19] We generally consider ourselves "rich" in direct proportion to how much we have compared to our neighbors.[20] When we compare downward, and see people who have less, we feel better about ourselves. When we compare upward, we feel worse. It turns out that we compare upward much more often than downward! In the United States, 40 percent of *millionaires* do not consider themselves wealthy. More than half of those worth more than $25 million consider themselves financially insecure. As one journalist wrote, "How wealthy one *feels* is often only moderately related to how wealthy one *is*."[21] While that is not true in all cases, chances are good that it is true for you.

Four ancient rabbis each had a different way of teaching about the subjectivity of wealth. Rabbi Akiva, who was born poor but who married a wealthy woman, describes wealth as having more money and possessions than you will ever use. Rabbi Meir, himself a scribe, considers as "wealthy" anyone who gleans joy from whatever they have. His contemporary, Rabbi Tarfon, a wealthy social-justice activist, teaches that a "wealthy" person is someone with a pleasant partner with whom to share a life. Rabbi Yossi was a tanner, a trade held in contempt; he connected wealth to the comfort of one's house by teaching that a wealthy person is "anyone who has a bathroom close to one's table."[22] The diversity of belief itself indicates that "wealth" is in the eye of the beholder.

While there is disagreement about what constitutes wealth, there is near-universal agreement in Judaism that a person can grow to love money so much that it gets in the way of the rest of their life. Judaism has always understood that when it comes to money, humans need to be careful. Money is a tactic, not a goal. It is meant to make life better for you and your community; it is not meant to be an orienting principle for existence.[23]

The inclination to worship money is sharply intensified by our consumerist culture in which market economics only works if you feel like you never have enough. I once read that the average person in the United States sees more than three thousand advertisements *every single day*, more in one day than people fifty years ago saw in a lifetime. The journalist noted that this means that "3,000 times a day, we're told that our hair is wrong, our skin is wrong, our clothes are wrong, our furniture is wrong, our cars are wrong, we are wrong but that it can all be made right if we just go shopping."[24] If having more stuff made us happier, then the United States would be the happiest nation on Earth. Instead, it is twenty-third, after countries like Costa Rica and New Zealand, where there are far fewer resources per person.[25]

Loving money too much leads to the belief that you can never have enough. When we spend too much time comparing ourselves to others and mired in not-enoughness, the consequences can be dire. We all know people for whom the *lack* of money causes them to lie awake at night. Judaism teaches that *too much* money, especially money hoarded uselessly, can do the same thing. It's better to work hard and be generous. That way, if the money evaporates in some "unlucky venture," your family will still have a way to survive. You will have people you can lean on for financial gifts, and you will have a trade that can help you begin to rebuild.[26]

What do I do with my money?

I was eighteen years old when I gave my first gift to *tzedakah*, a word often translated as "charity," but which actually means "justice through money." My tzedakah was to a microfunding organization called the Ziv Tzedakah Fund, led by Rabbi Danny Siegel. Danny traveled the United States and Israel looking for individuals or tiny, grassroots organizations that directly impacted communities in need. He would give money to those who had no way to widely publicize their work. This was before the internet, so without people like Danny, there was little way for a small organization to become known.

I took out my brand-new checkbook and wrote out the check for $18, an auspicious number in Judaism. Each Hebrew letter has a numerical value. The value of the letters in the Hebrew word "chai," or "life," add up to the number eighteen. Often, when Jews give tzedakah or gifts of money, they will do it in multiples of eighteen, a hat-tip to the belief that life is the most important value of all.

I handed the check to Danny, expecting a thank you, some genuflection, and perhaps a marching band. Was he not *so lucky* to be the recipient of my beneficence? Instead, he looked me dead in the eye and said, "Mazel tov," congratulations, an expression typically used when someone gets married or has a baby. By saying "mazel tov," and not "thank you," Danny was letting me know that he was *not* grateful to me for my gift. He thought that *I* was the lucky one. I got to give away my money, my tzedakah![27] I was stunned.

Danny's mazel tov really turned the tables for me on the values underlying tzedakah. When I give away "my" money (which is not entirely mine to begin with), I am fulfilling a responsibility. This understanding is definitionally distinct from the word "charity," which comes from the Latin "caritas," or "love," and is understood as something we do from the goodness of our heart. For Danny Siegel—and for the concept of tzedakah in general—goodness and love come second. Responsibility comes first.

In Judaism, giving tzedakah is more akin to the process of paying taxes than to that of giving gifts. We are asked to give away between 10 and 20 percent of our income each year. That money can go to many kinds of not-for-profit, charitable, or religious institutions, or an individual person in need.

Giving away a percentage of income, rather than a set amount, has many benefits. If your income goes down, while the total amount you give will be affected, your percentage doesn't need to be. If your income goes up, you have no excuse not to increase your giving. It also addresses a pet peeve of mine, which is that the rich get credit for giving more money when they *have* more money to give. Shouldn't the *poor* get more credit for giving money, since their giving represents a higher percentage of their income?

I have offered a few reasons for giving tzedakah. For one, the money is not ours to begin with, so some of it needs to be distributed more widely. For another, tzedakah can right injustice and help make the world a fairer place to live. Giving tzedakah is not only understood as a selfless act. While Jewish tradition would prefer for people to do the right thing for the right reason, it is acceptable to do the right thing for reasons that are not entirely altruistic.

My favorite piece of jewelry is a gold pin, about as tall as my thumb, depicting a roaring lion holding a Jewish star. I am not someone who wears a lot of jewelry, and even if I did, the aesthetics of this pin do not match mine. This is nevertheless the piece of jewelry that I will be most proud to pass on to my children. The pin depicts the "Lion of Judah." It represents membership in the women's philanthropic arm of the Jewish Federations of North America. When I wear it, I am announcing that I make a gift of at least $5,000 annually to my local chapter of JFNA, the umbrella organization that supports all sorts of Jewish organizations, which in turn support all kinds of people and great causes. I am not humble; I am showing off that I give tzedakah.

Some people dislike the pin, because they feel that it is bragging or ostentatious— seriously, a *gold* pin of a lion, with a diamond-chip eye, no less, that indicates I have given money to people in poverty? Gauche. I understand their point of view; I, too, wish we lived in a world where everyone gave a minimum of 10 percent of their money to tzedakah and didn't feel the need to talk about it. But Judaism invites us to do our work in the real world, rather than an imagined, ideal one. In the real world, human nature includes emotions like pride. When I wear my lion pin, I want people to know that I give tzedakah. When other people see it, they may be inspired to do the same.

Giving away money changes how we feel about ourselves. It changes our brain, lighting up what is called the reward system, giving us energy and pleasure. Research shows that giving away money makes us happier,[28] even happier than buying things for ourselves.[29] When we give tzedakah, we sometimes get a direct or indirect benefit. If you give money to your kids' private school for financial aid, for example, your children will benefit from whichever students are now able to attend the school. Fewer people in poverty means lower crime rates.[30] While your tzedakah should not be driven by self-interest, it is entirely acceptable to reap some benefits. For example: Anyone who purchases one of the more than two hundred million boxes of Girl Scout cookies sold per year can apply 54 percent of the cost of the cookies to tzedakah![31]

For many of us, giving away 10 percent of our net income is an onerous burden. I understand if 10 percent feels like a dream; that is true for most of the people with whom I've worked. But just because you cannot give 10 percent does not mean that you give nothing. Every dollar, every starfish, makes a difference. Consider the following step-by-step plan, which can help you increase your giving gradually and steadily.

STEP 1

Figure out . . .

1. How much money you gave to tzedakah over the past 12 months. Take into account all of the following.

   a. Money you gave to family members in need, not including typical holiday or birthday cash gifts

   b. Every crowdfunding drive, school fundraiser, donation to people on the street, or other informal giving, such as buying backpacks and filling them with school supplies for kids who need them

2. How much money you took home during the same time period.

3. What percentage #1 is of #2.

This gives you a baseline tzedakah percentage, a starting point from which to progress.

STEP 2

Create a document in which to write down every dollar that you will give to tzedakah this year. Include the following columns.

1. Name of organization

2. Area of giving (for example: mutual aid, hunger, advocacy)

3. For those who take deductions: Was the gift tax-deductible? If so, where is the receipt?

4. Other notes. I find this last column helpful because sometimes the "name of organization" is Target or my local bookstore and I have to remember that this money was used to purchase supplies for a local school in need.

STEP 3

Have a sit-down with the people in your family with whom you typically make financial decisions.

1. Present all the information you have gathered so far.

2. Determine whether you can increase the percentage point this year.

3. Set metrics for how and when you are going to increase the percentage of money you give to tzedakah. (When you get a bonus? Cost-of-living raise?)

4. Think about which categories you want to support with your tzedakah. Shelter for the unhoused? International aid? A political party whose candidates you believe will help alleviate poverty? While, on a very technical level, some of these categories might not count as tzedakah according to the strictest interpretations of Jewish law, for our purposes they certainly suffice. Set a percentage that you want to give in each of those areas and try to stick to it over the year. This will help you avoid giving to causes, out of a sense of obligation, that are not actually critical to you, or because end-of-year appeals end up in your email inbox.

5. If you like to give to friends who are raising money for causes dear to them, even if these causes are not close to your heart, make sure to set aside a small percentage of tzedakah for them.

6. Set a date on which you want to make sure that all your tzedakah has been given for the year. Some people use Rosh Hashanah (the Jewish New Year) as that date. In my family, we chose December 31, because it's the end of the tax year.

STEP 4

Give it away!

What if I want to volunteer instead of giving tzedakah?

While volunteering gets an enthusiastic thumbs-up in Judaism, it falls in the category of chesed, not tzedakah. It's like saying, "Should I compost or be nice to people?" They are both wonderful, and both good for the world, in very different ways.

Research does show that volunteering is a philanthropic driver; that the more personal connection a person has with an organization, the more money they will give.[32] But volunteering often does more to support the *volunteer's* spiritual or emotional development than it does for the organization itself. Think about all those volunteers who go to developing nations to help build latrines. We can all agree that it would be more cost-efficient if they sent the cash spent on the trip, such as airfare, lodging, food, special clothing, and let locals hire local latrine builders to do the work. So do both: Give of your time *and* your money.

Can I include donated clothing as part of my 10 percent?

If you give away brand-new clothes that have been specifically requested by people in need, yes. If you are giving away used clothing or used furniture or other home goods that you no longer want, then it does not count as tzedakah. It is still a good deed—also chesed—but a different category. (If you were planning to sell the items instead of donating them, then the resale value of the clothing could be counted as tzedakah.)

What do I do with the other 80–90 percent of my income?

Most of our non-tzedakah money will go to housing, food, savings, and other basic needs. Often there is something left over for enjoyment—for travel, restaurant meals, or new boots. When there is disposable income after taxes, basic needs, and tzedakah, Judaism says: Go for it! One Jewish teaching says that when we die, we will be held accountable for all the good food we saw in the world and did *not* taste.[33] We are meant to enjoy life, including using our money to do so.

We also can use our "leftover" money to take the good we do in the world and beautify it. This tradition, *hiddur mitzvah*, loosely translated as "beautifying a mitzvah," encourages us to spend disposable income on elevating our values with our purchasing power. Consider the important traditions of welcoming guests, honoring parents, or taking care of animals. You might "beautify" these values by upgrading your dining room so you can welcome the largest number of people possible for meals, or by taking your parents on vacation, or by adopting an elderly dog from a shelter, even though you know it will cost more money to keep it healthy than it would a puppy.

To use "God talk" one more time: A precept of Judaism is to love God with our hearts and souls and also with our money.[34] To the greatest extent possible, every single dollar we spend should be used ethically and in a "godly" manner. In Judaism, a spiritual practice is not just about conversations between us and God. It is about how we behave every single hour of the day. If we let our values guide us in choosing what to buy—and what not to—we can build a more holy world.

Tradition provides numerous other ways to use our discretionary income to make the world a better place. We are instructed to use our purchasing power to buy goods produced ethically, even when that means spending more, which it often does. It's forbidden to go into a store to get information on items sold there if you are sure that you are going to find the same item cheaper elsewhere, a type of window-shopping that has greatly intensified in the internet era.[35] It is forbidden to make your purchases from a business that you know treats its workers poorly, or to buy meat from farms where animals were treated unethically while they were alive. Saving money at the expense of human or animal lives, or of their dignity, or of the environment is illegal, according to Jewish tradition.

So, spend your money, but do it ethically, and only to a point. In medieval Jewish history, there were so-called "sumptuary" laws to keep people from being ostentatious in the way they spent their money. Rabbis set limits on how much money could be spent at life-cycle events, like weddings and funerals, so as not to engender competition that would lead people to bankrupt themselves. There were concerns around wastefulness, even hundreds of years before disposable cutlery. The rabbis were also worried that too many over-the-top events would increase antisemitism.

When it came to excessive behavior, ancient rabbis were especially worried about our political leaders. Rulers were forbidden to accumulate too much money, too many objects, and also too many wives! There was a fear that the more money rulers had, the more greedy they would become, and the less able to connect with regular folk, and with the poor and needy.[36]

The ethics and values of Judaism are meant to be institutionalized not only in the synagogue and in the home, but also on the street and in one's place of business. In Judaism, the accumulation of money *can* be good, but only when it is being earned, saved, and disbursed in ways that are wise and humble, and infused with strong values.[37] Using our money thoughtfully, in support of gaining joy from the world and building a more fair world, helps us live a meaningful life every day.

Chapter 6

The Way of
Limud: Education

Imagine a large room in which dozens of people sit at tables, gesticulating wildly at those who sit across from them. Open books are splayed all around. The tables are stacked with more books; overflowing bookshelves line the walls. At the front of the room is a lectern at which, from time to time, a teacher stands. Much of the time, the teacher roams the room assisting students as they pour over the texts, in pairs or sometimes groups of three, in a core relationship called *chevruta* ("learning partner"). Students sometimes raise their voices. The room is noisy and may seem chaotic or disorganized.

Welcome to a yeshiva ("place of sitting"), an academy of Jewish learning. These institutions don't look very different today from centuries ago, aside from their expansion to include people of all genders and not only men. Students and their teachers often practice specific, millennia-old learning protocols. A unifying principle of this type of learning is that the highest honor you can pay someone is to challenge their ideas, which makes both of you smarter. Chevrutas believe the other person worthy of their ideas and believe themselves worthy of voicing their own.

Learning is one of the most important values in the Jewish tradition. It is one of the most important methodologies for understanding what it is that God demands of us in the world. When a sacred book falls on the floor, we pick it up and kiss it, as if to apologize for the indignity of something so important falling to the ground. If someone drops a Torah scroll, everyone Jewish who sees it drop is supposed to fast for *forty* days, although they can eat at night. This is a physical representation of repentance for the "sin" of disrespecting our most important book.

Jewish dedication to learning in religious contexts bleeds into a drive for learning in secular subjects, as well. More than half of all Jewish adults (59 percent) have attained a college degree, compared to 29 percent in the general United States population; 25 percent have earned a graduate degree, compared to 6 percent of all Americans.[1] Around the Jewish dinner table, one often hears advice like, "Your education is the only thing that can't be taken away from you."

One of my favorite stories about Jews and books comes from my family's move from Philadelphia to Washington, DC. The movers arrived from a rural area where our boxes had been in storage. One of the men came up to me and said, "Excuse me, ma'am? I'm sorry to tell you that someone wrote 'Jew books' all over many of your boxes." He thought it was antisemitic graffiti, but I quickly eased his worry. "Oh, yes," I replied. "That was me."

We were moving into our home right before the Jewish High Holidays, a time when I write a lot of sermons and need access to my Jewish books. I explained to the mover that I had written these labels so these specific boxes would be easier to find. And the conversation continued. First, we spoke about the fact that the word "Jew" is not an epithet. But mostly we talked about the dozens of boxes of books that the movers were unloading. I told him about one of my favorite articles by Rabbi Vanessa Ochs, in which she writes that one of the signifiers of a Jewish home is "books, some of which might be by Jews or about Judaism—but also all books in abundance, filling shelves, piled on floors, spilling off tables, scattered in children's rooms."[2] He told me that his coworkers fought *not* to get assigned our job, not because of antisemitism but because there were so many heavy boxes of books! I learned a lot about how movers do their jobs, and he learned a lot about Jewish culture and values.

People of the Book

Why is it that Jews are called "People of the Book"? Why is it that even the most secular of Jews still feel so deeply connected to learning, even if not necessarily on Jewish topics? One reason is that there is a correlation between education and income. Upwardly mobile Jews know that people with professional degrees make on average three times the amount of money as those who did not graduate from high school.[3] Perhaps more important, education, which is mostly portable, helps people get a professional foothold if they are forced to move from one place to another.

But it is not just about the money. Significant numbers of people learn without a thought to any future remuneration, and others endure years of schooling only to take relatively lower-paying jobs as social workers, public defenders, or professors. For Jews, education is a life-orientation. We are a People of Learners, and this impacts how we see ourselves, others, and the world around us. For Jews, "learning" does not only describe an activity; it is an approach to life.

The methodology of education, Jewish-style, has not changed significantly over the last three thousand years. What does Judaism have to teach about how to learn?

Have deep relationships with fellow learners

Chevruta, or partnered learning, with its characteristic batting of an idea back and forth, deepens our understanding and overall information retention. When we work with another person to peel back the layers of a problem or idea, we better understand the principles on which it stands, the straw men that others may use to try to tear it down, and the valid arguments to counter them.

In a contemporary Jewish learning environment, each person would have a copy of the text they are learning in front of them. The text is usually in Hebrew, although it could be in Yiddish, Aramaic, Arabic, English, or in whatever vernacular the students know best. One of the partners reads aloud, the pair translates if necessary, and then they wrestle with the meaning and implications of the text they just read.

Dr. Orit Kent and Allison Cook teach that there are three partners in every chevruta: two people and the text. "Listening and articulating are at the heart of chevruta learning," they continue. "We strive to support and challenge ourselves, our partner, and the text, as we eschew the simplistic goal of advocating our position and instead help all three partners 'speak' to develop the strongest ideas."[4]

Like a three-legged stool, our learning could collapse if any one leg were missing. If it's just me and the text without my chevruta, I risk not fully understanding the implications of the text nor being able to hear other opinions on it. As one rabbi said thousands of years ago: "[With my chevruta], when I would state a matter, he would raise twenty-four difficulties against me [in an attempt to disprove my claim], and I would answer him with twenty-four answers, and the law by itself would become broadened [and clarified]."[5] When all three legs are sturdy, however, we learn something new through our own lens, through the life experience of our chevruta, and through our ancestors who studied these same texts millennia ago. The chevruta relationship can last for an hour or a lifetime. We bring its teachings, both overt and subconscious, back with us into the rest of our lives.

Wisdom, learning, and knowledge don't come by osmosis. When we study Jewish texts, we enter into conversation with all those who have come before us. In traditional circles, the earlier a text was written, the more weight it will be given in the conversation.

When I study, then, I'm arguing not just with my chevruta but also with whoever wrote the text we are learning. If we take these texts seriously, we can imagine that in a hundred or a thousand years another chevruta will be arguing about *our* ideas. Rabbi Abraham Isaac Kook wrote that Judaism succeeds because we have the ability to make the old new, and the new holy. The texts we read are our inheritance. Our own insights will be our legacy.

When we engage in Jewish text study together, whether with texts composed thousands of years ago or with contemporary works, we honor Jewish tradition and ourselves. Our voices are made important as we add them to the ongoing Jewish conversation. The text becomes the "third space" through which we have a conversation about creating a life of meaning. There is no obligation to agree with the arguments made on the page or by our chevruta. There *is* an obligation to listen, consider, and engage in mostly respectful dialogue.

Disagreement is good

A few years ago, my family spent a week in Idaho, kayaking the middle fork of the Salmon River. One morning, we unexpectedly found ourselves heading toward a forest fire. When our guides saw what was coming downriver, they pulled us aside and said, "We're going to go around the bend and find ourselves in the middle of a forest fire. Here's what we're going to do: We're going to crack open a six-pack of calm, and then paddle like there's a python behind us. Stay in the middle of the river. Go." River guides actually talk like this.

That's what we did. We paddled through the fire, trees burning on the banks on both sides of us, brush aflame, branches loudly crackling off trees and falling into the water. Although we passed through the fire for only a few minutes, it felt like forever, and then it was over. "It's cool now," the guides said. "As you were."

The next night, over dinner in the camp, our guides taught us about what it takes for a fire to erupt. Did you know, they said, that fire can travel slowly, underground, for weeks, jumping from root to root, before it rises aboveground? They taught us that technology is being devised to sense when the pressure is building underground, so as to avert a full-fledged fire.

When it comes to human discourse, we already have this technology; it's called *being in conversation*. There's a war being fought right now, not between the progressive left and the alt-right, or between red states and blue states, or between the rich and the poor. It's between those who are willing to sit in disagreement with the perceived other and those who are not.

Two thousand years ago, Jews were divided into groups called the Sadducees, Pharisees, and Essenes. The groups hated each other, couldn't speak with each other, were embarrassed by the views that the others held. Our tradition teaches that this hatred led to the destruction of the second Temple and the exile of the majority of the Jews from the land of Israel. From the ashes of exile, a new group was created, one that would welcome other members if they learned the rules of engagement and agreed to disagree with each other. This group was called "the rabbis."

Together, the rabbis created a series of books called the Talmud, which contains five thousand arguments, only fifty of which were fully resolved.[6] One percent. It turns out that the rabbis' goal was not to come to particular resolutions but to be in conversation across difference, to attempt to prove their own points, and to hear and learn from the perspectives of others. The rabbis honed the art of conversation over many centuries with sharp questions, curiosity, and a drive for truth.

These rabbis' arguments didn't last a week, or a month, or even a year. If you were to read a page of Talmud and see Rabbi X arguing a point with Rabbi Y, you'd need to keep in mind that they may have lived *hundreds* of years apart from each other. These arguments continued over lifetimes and beyond. Fires take weeks to rise up; they can't be smothered in an hour. The Talmudic rabbis, as they argued and even called each other insulting names, stayed in relationship. What if we could do that, too?

One casualty of our aversion to talking to anyone different from us is that we don't learn how to have difficult conversations. We can learn from the trees, which, over the millennia, have developed "adaptations that allow them to survive easier in natural fire."[7] If we *practice* talking to other people, we learn how to do it in real time. In Hebrew, this practice is called *machloket*, conversation across difference.

Unlike the trees' resilience, talking across difference does not come naturally. It takes skill building and practice. We must practice the art of reflective listening. When someone voices an opinion that you strongly disagree with, what is your initial instinct? To wait for their lips to stop moving so you can argue your point? Or maybe to interrupt them? To tune them out altogether and start making a shopping list in your mind? To immediately place this person in the category of "not worth my time"?

What might it feel like to actively listen to what the person is saying? As they are talking, to try to truly understand? And when they are done, to reflect it back to them? "I hear you saying X. Did I get that right?" Questions like this will help the speaker feel truly heard, and therefore encourage them to listen to you. It may also help them refine their thinking in real time, ensuring that they mean what they say. It will help you, the listener, not to jump to conclusions based on the first few words of the speaker's sentences.

Another strategy for having conversations across difference is to ask clarifying questions. Why do you think that? Did anything happen in your life that makes you more likely to think this? What do you think the implications would be if that happened? Or: I disagree with this one thing you said; would you be interested in hearing why that is? Remember, the goal is not to change anyone's mind but to understand why they believe what they believe.

Even when we *do* have the goal of changing people's minds, we should still begin with a listening and curious posture. Research has shown that there are a few ways to change people's minds. One of them is to tell your own personal story, and another is to listen to theirs.[8] Other researchers have suggested that our own thinking has always evolved with the goal of relationality rather than objectivity.[9] In order to convince others, we need to connect.

On the river, our guides taught us that we need to permit small-scale forest fires in order to avoid the larger conflagrations. The same is true for human disagreements. When we are in a state of machloket, Jewish tradition encourages us to let the fire rise, just a little bit. We are urged to listen for comprehension, be reflective enough to realize when we do not know as much as we thought we did, notice when our blood pressure is rising, understand that this will not help us learn, and practice calming skills like deep breathing. It can be exhausting, but it works. We allow the fire to rise a few inches above the ground and we clear away the brush. We are not starting a conflagration.

The ancient rabbis knew that the stakes of disagreements can be high, and that when we do a bad job of disagreeing with one another we can destroy relationships. The Talmud gives the example of Rabbi Eliezer, who, after being mistreated and exiled by his colleagues over what started off as a relatively minor disagreement, caused literal fires with his angry gaze.[10] There is a balance to be had in disagreeing with others.

Every moment isn't identical when we're talking about conversations across difference. Sometimes "the Other" really is just that; someone who, mired in their hatred, will never change. They, like the generation of Israelites redeemed from slavery, will die in the desert. But don't focus too much on them, because there are also millions of people who *are* open to conversation. Find them, then find the moments in which deep conversation can happen. Jack pines have cones that can't open to release seeds without a fire—they need a certain heat to open up. Like most seeds, they may not grow into healthy trees or thriving forests for generations, but we can't worry about that. All we can do is release the seeds so that they might be planted.

The world is burning, but it is also lit up with beauty, which can be found in the surfacing of difficult conversations. As we paddle a river that flows for thousands of miles beyond this fire immediately in front of us, we need to crack open a six-pack of calm and model the ancient Jewish art of nuanced, slow-moving, thoughtful conversation.

Parents have a responsibility to teach their children

I was thirty-five years old before I learned that some parents, including loving ones who otherwise care for their children in all ways, don't think it's their responsibility to ensure that their children receive an excellent education.

I was sitting in my office in Washington, DC, talking to a young woman named Madison about her childhood. "My parents really loved me," she said. "I had food on the table and clothes on my back." Madison graduated from high school without having had any conversations at all about college or career training. She was welcome to stay in her parents' home for as long as she wanted, rent free. Her parents would not give her any more of their money, nor did they offer any advice on what she should do next. It was entirely up to her, at eighteen, to make her way in the world.

This is very different from how I grew up, and how I parent. My grandparents and great-grandparents immigrated to the United States; none of them went to college. They did blue-collar work all their lives with the goal of their children attending college and graduate school. They raised their children—and my parents raised me and my brothers—to "do better" than they did, by which they sometimes meant "make more money," but always meant "get more education."

From a young age, it was never a question of *whether* I would go to college but *where*. My parents scrimped and saved and helped me pay for college by living in a simpler home than many of the people in our community, driving older, beat-up cars, and not taking many vacations. They cared for my small children while I was in graduate school so that I could study. When each of my children was born, the first thing we did was set up a 529 plan (authorized by Section 529 of the Internal Revenue Code) so that with every birthday and every Hanukkah, we could put a little money aside for their college education.

My parents did not love me any more than Madison's parents love her. They had different values, and those values had trickled down through the generations. Judaism holds that educating one's children is a primary parental responsibility. We believe that the more learning there is in the world, the more peace there will be, and that our children will build a better world to benefit all of us.[11] We often take much more pleasure and pride in our children's achievements than in our own.

According to the Talmud, Jewish parents have a few very specific obligations.

1. Commit to raising their children as Jews.

2. Teach their children the Jewish story, ethics, and values.

3. Help them find a life-partner.

4. Teach them a trade.

5. Some say, teach them to swim—that is, give them life skills.[12]

This text, in its original form, was written about fathers and sons. I have taken the liberty of making it more gender-inclusive, hopeful that, had the ancient rabbis lived in the twenty-first century, they would have been in favor of gender egalitarianism!

According to this list, more than 50 percent of a parent's job is educating their child. Having a productive trade is considered a necessity for enjoying life. If a parent does *not* make sure that their child learns a trade, it is as if they are content with their child's becoming a thief.[13]

Madison became an aesthetician, a career of which she was very proud, but she wanted to create a different culture from the one in her childhood home. She wanted her two sons to be aware of a wider variety of options than she had upon graduating from high school. She frequented the library and read to her kids whenever she had a few moments at the end of a long day of work. She and her children listened to kids' science podcasts when they were in the car. She moved her family to a tiny apartment in a neighborhood with better schools; she joined the PTA. When her children complained that other people at their school went on fancy vacations, while their family did not, she reminded them that their family's primary value was education, and everything else came second. Most important of all, she started asking for help from other parents who worked fewer hours or who knew more about extracurricular offerings than she did. She swallowed her pride and asked about scholarships for her children, and they often received them.

Today, Madison's two sons are in high school. It is not clear what their specific trades will be, but Madison has made her family's values clear. Madison built upon thousands of years of Jewish tradition and contemporary Jewish culture and pushed her children toward education.

The community has a responsibility to teach all children

When Madison decided to change the family culture in her generation, she was heartened to learn she was not alone. Children's education cannot happen in a vacuum, nor can any one parent or even one family system shoulder the entire burden of education. It is the entire community's responsibility to educate children, including adults with no children of their own. Communal responsibility for education is such a critical value that one of the most well-respected rabbis in all of Jewish history taught that there should be teachers in every single village, and that if a town does not have a school, the townspeople should be excommunicated from the rest of the Jewish community until they hire someone to teach. "If they do not employ teachers, the village deserves to be destroyed," Maimonides taught a thousand years ago, "since the world exists only by virtue of the breath coming from the mouths of children."[14]

There is a metaphorical understanding that a town without education for its children is destroying its own future. Contemporary research holds this to be true. A lack of teachers and education impacts not only the children who do not receive education but also their family members and the larger community. The less education, the more crime and poverty. Poverty may not affect us all, but increased crime certainly does.[15]

I have heard many people without children complain about having to pay taxes to support public schools that they do not utilize. They argue that while *everyone* needs city services like police and fire departments, not everyone needs schools, and only those who need them should have to pay for them. The Jewish approach is similar to American law, however, which holds that every young person has the right to education, and that it is the community's responsibility to pay for it.[16] Community-sponsored education is supposed to start at age five and continue until age twenty.[17] When everyone has access, our collective wisdom grows. The Talmud relates a story of a coup in the Beit Midrash, the rabbinic house of study, where the guards at the door were removed and people flooded in to learn. The story says that thousands of words of sacred learning were recorded on that one day.[18] In Judaism, schools are so important that neighbors are forbidden to protest when a school opens in their backyard![19]

Children should be seen AND heard

Many of us grew up in a culture that believed adults should be obeyed without question. Judaism mostly holds the opposite. Children are taught to respect their elders by asking good questions, which is considered a sign of respect. The entire posture of the Passover seder, the annual ritual dinner at which we recall the Israelite exodus from Egypt, is based on the premise that children must ask questions in order for them, and for adults, to learn. A very famous tale of four rabbis arguing with each other ends with the rabbis disagreeing with God, and God allowing the rabbis to win! God shakes God's (metaphorical) head, repeating with a (metaphorical) proud smile, "My children have defeated me, my children have defeated me!"[20]

Isidor I. Rabi, a Nobel laureate in physics, was once asked why he became a scientist, and not a businessman like other immigrant kids in his neighborhood. "My mother made me a scientist without ever intending it," he answered. "Every other Jewish mother in Brooklyn would ask her child after school: 'So? Did you learn anything today?' But not my mother. She always asked me a different question. 'Izzy,' she would say, 'did you ask a good question today?' That difference—asking good questions—made me become a scientist!"[21]

Here we see evidence not only of a parent taking responsibility for their child's education but also the importance of learning *and* of curiosity. The second-best question is, "What did you learn?" And the best question is, "Did you ask a good question?" In some cultures, children asking too many questions or those that are too challenging is considered disrespectful. In Judaism, it is the highest honor. A core teaching argues that the wise person learns from everyone, no matter what their age.[22]

Book learning does not end when you finish school

Learning is not only for children. It starts in the womb,[23] and continues until we die. A Jewish tale teaches that every fetus learns the entirety of the Torah—which we can read broadly as learning everything that is most important—in utero. As children emerge into the world, an angel taps them above the mouth and they forget all they have learned, ready to start a lifetime of (re)learning.

Every day of our lives, no matter our age, job, or level of education, we are expected to set aside time for learning something new.[24] A number of reasons are given for our discipline of lifelong learning. Continued learning is good for the brain and prevents cognitive decline. One study of people ages fifty-eight to eighty-six showed that taking classes later in life very quickly leads to brain functioning that looks more like someone at least *thirty* years younger than their chronological age.[25] Learning new skills is also associated with a decrease in dementia.[26]

Here's what I have to say to the 45 percent of older adults who report rarely learning something new: Why? Consider lifelong learning. It will make whatever years you have left more interesting and enjoyable. Learning new things will help you have better conversations with loved ones, leading to even more of a legacy even after your death.

In Judaism, we are supposed to look at texts *as if* they are new, even if we have been studying them all our lives. We read selected biblical passages once a year, and then start all over again. Some people study one page of Talmud a day for seven years to complete this massive compendium of Jewish knowledge. When the seven years are done, they start again. What is it that makes these practices meaningful?

The words stay the same, but we change, and the world around us changes. As we evolve, we uncover whole new meanings in the ancient texts. Jewish study asks us to bring our lived experience to the text, and our experience grows over the course of a lifetime. We read the same texts differently at the ages of eleven, fifty-one, and ninety-one. The overlay of our own lived experiences can transform a text that we have already read a dozen times. If we become parents, for instance, we may read the stories of our ancestors Isaac and Rebecca's treatment of their twins Jacob and Esau differently. Or when we are near the end of our lives, we can learn about aging by reading the story of our ancestor Moses's death. If we had read the text only once and then never again, we would have taken in only some of what these stories have to offer.

Adult learning is also important because our kids are watching. When Madison and I started meeting, we often began with a short chevruta, a study of a text. I encouraged her to go home and tell her sons about what we learned together, modeling that she not only expected *them* to learn about Judaism but that she also had expectations of herself. Madison later took classes toward her real estate license and then obtained it. We celebrated that day.

Some of us have more bandwidth to continue our studies than others. We may be exhausted after a long day of work, unable even to imagine taking the time to learn something new. If that is the case for you, just do your best. Here, technology can be your friend. Listen to one podcast, read one article on your phone, take one class online or at the local community center. Talk about your learning with your partner, friends, or children. Learning does not have to be formal to be effective.

No one is "not smart enough" to learn

Long before IQ tests or Individualized Education Plans, Judaism recognized and appreciated differences in learning styles and interests. When we meet someone who is differently abled, we are instructed to offer a blessing of gratitude for the fact that all of humanity is created differently.[27]

It is the parent or the teacher's responsibility—not the student's—to make sure the student learns. An old proverb reads, "If you teach a child according to their way, they will not forget what they learned, even in their old age."[28] Educators are forbidden to place any "stumbling blocks" in the way of students to keep them from advancing in their studies. The Talmud teaches that people whose parents don't educate them have to educate themselves, taking on accountability for their own development.[29]

What are students supposed to learn? Enough so that they can be gainfully employed and have an operational set of ethics and values. Enough so that they can fully participate in the community, which may mean participating in civic society (jury duty, voting, basic neighborliness). Parents, teachers, and students have some leeway about what to learn but not about whether they must learn.

Learning does not *have* to be goal oriented, but it's encouraged

Throughout this book, I refer to a number of words as being "so that" words. The word "zachor," or memory, translates as "remember so that." Chesed is "love-in-action," or "kindness so that." The "so that" theory is true for *limud*, or learning, as well.

A few thousand years ago, a group of rabbis were hanging out when a question was posed to them: Which is greater, study or action? Rabbi Tarfon argued that the answer is action, because just sitting in a yeshiva studying all day is not going to heal this broken world. Another rabbi, Akiva, said that study is greater. The rest of the group agreed with Akiva, but with a caveat: that the study not be an end unto itself. Instead, "study is greater than action because it leads to action."[30] Text is a springboard, not a cul-de-sac. Study is the planning and forethought that makes action more effective. We learn *so that* learning can lead to action.

One ancient text teaches that anyone who holds the posture of lifelong learning for its own sake merits being called a "friend, beloved, lover of all creatures and the place they are in. These people are humble and hold a reverence for the universe." Lifelong learners are more prepared to be "righteous, devout, upright and trustworthy, and to misstep less often." They are "slower to anger and quicker to forgive." People tend to see this person as strong and understanding, and want this person's advice. These people are compared to "an ever-strengthening spring, and like a river that does not stop."[31] While this teaching has not been scientifically proven, I know people for whom it applies; you probably do, too.

"Learning" is different from other nouns because the "so that" quality is only part of the reason we learn. The goal of learning is not *always* to learn something that leads to action. Sometimes, learning is an end unto itself. The Jewish approach to learning is ultimately about opening the mind and heart to understanding more about ourselves, our community, our people, and the world. Our goal is to love studying, which includes our study partner and the ideas and discussions that arise between us. We aim to feel the joy that comes from being around people who are interested in deepening themselves and bettering the world, to find texts that inspire us, and to argue against those that infuriate us. Learning permits us to take our identities into our own hands and do our part to build a different, more enlightened future.

Chapter 7

The Way of *Am*: Community

A number of years ago, my congregant Lisa graduated from college and moved back home to DC, only to learn from her parents that they had sold their house and were moving to Florida. She felt abandoned. For the first time, she was living an adult life and afraid in the most existential way: She felt lonely.

In response, she did what many well-educated, thoughtful, contemporary twenty-somethings do: She got a tattoo. In Hebrew. *L'olam lo l'vad*, it says. Never alone. When she got the tattoo, it was perhaps an aspirational statement. With a lot of hard work on her part, it has come true.

Three years after her parents moved, Lisa got married. Her wedding was in Florida, and a planeload of people came down from DC. Most of them were what Lisa now calls her "DC family," the friends she met at synagogue and traveled with to Israel, those who celebrate and mourn together, and who love each other deeply, even in those moments when they do not *like* each other very much. At her wedding ceremony, when she lifted her arm to drink from the celebratory cup of wine, you could just about make out the words *l'olam lo l'vad*. Never alone.

A few years ago, in DC, we celebrated the baby naming of Lisa's daughter, the newest link in the chain. At the baby naming, Lisa was dressed modestly, so we could not see the tattoo, but it was there. She and her husband truly were not alone. They were surrounded by many of the same people who had stood with her at her wedding a few years before. "Never alone."

Building and participating in community is one of Judaism's most important values. Jewish texts teach that "if a person . . . secludes themself in the corner of their home and declares: 'What concerns are the problems of the community to me? What does their judgment mean to me? Why should I listen to them? I will do well [without them],' they help to destroy the world."[32] Or "Do not separate yourself from the community."

I learned in rabbinical school that sometimes when our teachers repeat themselves it is because the idea they are illuminating is one of Judaism's core principles. Something so central to what it means to be a good human bears repeating.

This is true of texts about community. We are forbidden to say a number of Jewish prayers unless we are part of a *minyan*, a group of at least ten people. And while a minyan is itself not a community, in order to have access to a minyan, there needs to be a group of people who will step forward when the need arises. We cannot function in a world without community. Sadly, this wisdom flies in the face of our fractured and increasingly anomic society.

In Robert D. Putnam's now famous book *Bowling Alone*, he writes about an arc of disconnection between people that has only grown over the past two dozen years, arguing that Americans "have become increasingly disconnected from family, friends, neighbors, and our democratic structures." Putnam's premise is that having what he calls a "social network" matters. He doesn't define "network" the way we might. It's not your Facebook friends and it is likely not the baristas at your local coffee shop, even if you know each other by name. "Network" is not just what he terms "warm and cuddly feelings, but a wide variety of quite specific benefits . . . [that] flow from the trust, reciprocity, information, and cooperation associated with social networks." Social networks, according to Putnam, "translate an 'I' mentality into a 'we' mentality."[33]

In modern culture, the definition of the word "community" has expanded almost beyond recognition. Community has become more of a marketing tool than a technical term, an attempt to lure in lonely, unhappy, or generally dissatisfied people. Community is regularly applied to those who work out at the same gym, drink coffee at the same cafe, or listen to the same podcast.

A true community, according to my working definition, is a group of people who fulfill the following.

- Invest time, energy, and care building social connections with a select group of others

- Come together for a common goal or purpose and are willing to sacrifice in order to achieve that purpose
- Are diverse in abilities and needs, with the caveat that different communities are diverse in different ways
- Are connected by at least one through line, be it religious, geographic, cultural, political, or other point of reference
- Care about and feel a responsibility for each other, even if they don't always like each other or agree on all topics
- Are no more than one degree separated from everyone else in the community, by which I mean that if two people from the community meet for the first time, they can always find someone else from the community that they know in common
- May request but never require a financial buy-in order for someone to be included
- Gather in person from time to time, even if only every five or six years. Social media and virtual meeting *boosts* but does not *replace* physical connection

Each of these points may be disconcerting to some of you for one reason or another. Some people prefer to spend most of their time only with people they really like. I understand that, of course. But a true community requires various kinds of diversity, including race, economic, ability, intelligence, education, religious, political, and personality. While it's rare to have every single type of diversity in a community—a Jewish community will have mostly Jews, for example, or a community of alumni will have people who all graduated from the same college—there needs to be some diversity, otherwise what you probably have is a friendship group.

Friendship is of vital importance, of course, but it is distinct from community.

If a group requires (rather than requests) a financial investment in order to participate, it is not a community; it is a business. SoulCycle, CrossFit, and your local coffee shop, for example, can all offer opportunities for personal growth, and may be quite spiritually oriented, but they are not communities. True communities may need financial contributions—how else can the rabbi get paid, or the electricity stay on?—but they also recognize that not everyone can afford to make the same contribution and adjust their fees accordingly.

Judaism is not one community, by the way. We are thousands of loosely connected communities located the world over, oriented toward a similar way of life, premised on interdependence, not independence, as evidenced by the following parable. A person, sitting in a boat, begins to drill a hole underneath their seat. Fellow passengers protest. The driller is defiant: "Why does it matter to you that I am creating this hole? It's under my own seat, not yours!" The other passengers reply: "That is true, but when the water comes in, it will sink the whole boat and we will all drown."[34] Our actions affect not only our own selves.

Acknowledging our interdependence is countercultural in the United States, which has historically fostered a myth of individualism. I grew up with stories of the self-sufficient cowboy, roaming the plains. Did you also grow up with this image, of a guy and his trusty horse doing roping, making fences, keeping away the bad guys every day, on their own, by nightfall? Here's the poorly kept secret: The cowboy is a FICTION. Rebecca Solnit writes beautifully about this, teaching that "the archetype of the self-reliant individual . . . has its roots . . . in the imagined history of Cold War–era westerns. [In reality,] the American West was . . . crisscrossed by government-subsidized railroads and full of water projects and other enormous cooperative enterprises."[35] Interdependence, not the mythology of American rugged individualism.

"Pulling yourself up by your own bootstraps" is a fallacy, as a Jewish teacher named Hillel established thousands of years ago. In a famous quote that has been mistakenly attributed to Robert F. Kennedy, Ronald Reagan, Emma Watson, and, most recently, Ivanka Trump, Hillel taught: "If I am not for myself, who will be for me? If I am only for myself, what am I?"[36] These two orientations are dependent on one another. Humans are part of an ecosystem of caring for others, caring for ourselves, and having people who care for us.

Alienation, loneliness, and a sense of failure can arise from not having a community of people on whom to lean when times are tough. Ample research compiled by Vivek Murthy, the surgeon general of the United States under President Biden, has shown that we are living in a public health crisis of isolation and loneliness. We sometimes get confused about which interactions offer true connection and then are disappointed when that does not happen. We confuse social media interactions with actual connections. We confuse the base capitalist model of *purchasing* face time with another human being (our hairdressers, our personal trainers) with the communal model of *offering* and *receiving*, with *engaging* with other humans because our fates are intertwined, and not because of any purchasing power.

I used to have a preconceived notion of lonely people. Maybe blame it on Steve Martin's 1984 movie *The Lonely Guy*. I thought they were socially awkward, living alone, not having much interaction with others, and without a great sense of style. My years as a rabbi have proved how wrong I was.

Lonely people are young and old (more often the former than the latter), married or single, rich or poor. Those we might consider "socially awkward" are sometimes *less* lonely than those whom society may deem "cool" or "hip." People in the latter category can be so busy worrying about their status and being hyperselective about friends or groups that they don't find long-lasting, reciprocal, generous community.

Biologists think that the feeling we call "loneliness" evolved as a necessary imperative to make humans realize the importance of working together in groups. "Hunger" tells us when to eat, "pain" tells us when to take our hand off the hot stove, "loneliness" tells us that we need to cooperate with other human beings in order to survive in a harsh world.[37]

To be clear, there's a difference between being "alone" and being "lonely." Many of us have felt lonely even in a roomful of people; many of us spend lots of time alone but are not at all lonely. Unfortunately, our ancient texts often conflate the two, attributing the same implication to both words.

Jewish texts often teach that being alone is "not good." As the world is created, the Bible teaches, everything is described as "good." The Earth is good, the animals are good. The creation of people is *very* good. After six "good" days of creation, what's the first thing that's "not good"? For the human to be alone.

Married or partnered people generally report being less lonely than single people; studies also report that people in a lousy marriage are lonely at a much higher rate than single people with strong friend groups.[38] Even in the best marriages or the most connected family systems, there are moments of disconnection. One person cannot fill all of another person's needs, and when we live as if this were true, we risk destroying relationships that could otherwise be deeply meaningful and long-lasting. Being able to rely on others to fill whatever gaps exist in our primary relationships is another reason that being in community is good not just for the larger whole, but for each of us as individuals.

People in their twenties are the loneliest of all.[39] I have spent much of my career working with people in that age group, and I have come up with some hypotheses to explain their loneliness. For some, it is because they are very busy, whether at work, exercise, on social media, or partying. They don't realize that "busy" does not equal "connected," and they may be surprised when their expectations do not coincide with reality.

Some people in their twenties do not know what it takes to participate in an authentic community. They do not realize that building and sustaining a community takes as much time and energy as any other endeavor in our lives. We don't go to the gym once and then think that we are done for the rest of our lives. But when it comes to community, we have what in contemporary Hebrew slang is called a *magia li*, an I-deserve-it attitude. As a rabbi, I have found that people who show up at an event once or twice and are not immediately integrated into the community that sponsored it are surprised or even offended. These are not narcissists, they say; they are truly lovely people who want to be part of something. Why aren't they immediately welcomed and integrated? Aren't religious communities tasked with being compassionate to *all* of God's creations?

Unfortunately, religious communities are made up of actual *human beings*, with all of our petty selfishness. While people at synagogue, church, or mosque should, I hope, be more welcoming and inclusive than folks at your local bar, we should not expect them to be *radically* different from the average human. Aside from the human foibles of its members, the best communities have boundaries, and recognizing that makes it more obvious why it can take time to be welcomed in.

Community doesn't happen *to* you, community is something that you build and tend to, or it stagnates, withers, and sometimes dies. Becoming—and remaining—part of a community takes serious work. The connection muscle needs to be built up and maintained, which means not only looking out for yourself and the people you like best, but also looking out for others. That might mean calling people when you haven't seen them in a while, or fixing them up with friends if they're single and you know that they want to be partnered.

As with your romantic relationships, your profession, or your physical health, with the work of building community comes blessing. How wonderful it is to have people who know you and your story, to whom you don't have to explain yourself and your idiosyncrasies. Or people who know little about you but would support you if you were ill. People with whom you've fought and made up, with whom you share scars that make your connection tighter, people to dance at your wedding, to mourn at your loved ones' funerals. People you can call and say, "I'm feeling bleh. Will you sit on the couch with me and watch TV?" To experience community is to live the opposite of loneliness.

The following is Rabbi Shira's highly unscientific guide to how to find and build community.

Notice what is missing.

In Judaism, the *navon* is the person who is able to achieve insight, to learn from a life experience or from what they have heard or read.[40] Achieving insight is more difficult than we recognize. Wars have been fought because humans did not have insight into their own actions or those of others. For us as individuals it is sometimes difficult to notice a feeling, such as sadness or anger, and have insight into what is causing it: loneliness, boredom, or frustration, perhaps. With that in mind, the first step toward finding community is actually a pre-step: noticing that something is missing from your life and hypothesizing about what could help fill the void.

Do you feel intellectually undernourished? Are you spiritually or emotionally alone? Is there something you want for your family? Have you noticed a brokenness in the world that you want to help fix? Is there a craft or intellectual pursuit that calls to you? Do you want to have more fun or be challenged in a new way? Are you lonely? Write a list of what you're looking for, so that you can better discover the type of community you want and/or need.

For example, if you want spiritual nourishment, your local political action committee will probably not help. If you want intellectual stimulation, don't start with your local kickball club.

A few thousand years ago, a group of rabbis got together and created a list of the infrastructure that needed to be in place before someone could join the community, including, for example, a place to gather and a leader.[41] Since your needs will not be the same as people living in fifth-century Babylon, don't worry about what else was on the rabbis' list; make your own. The more specific, the better. Are you someone who likes an organization with history, or are you drawn to start-up energy? Do you want an intergenerational community? What kind of diversity is important? Do you want a group composed primarily of people of your racial, ethnic, or other identity-based group? A community close to home? Are you open to groups that meet mostly online? In your ideal world, how often would you engage with the community? How important is it that it involves food and/or drink?

Be discerning (be a navon!) in your search for a community, because you want it to be as long-lasting as possible. Keeping your list handy will help you find the group that is right for you at this time of your life.

Explore before committing.

Begin by looking for communities that already exist. Do you want to join a book club? Ask around: What book groups already exist? I just typed "book clubs Washington, DC" into an internet search and found lots of local bookstores and libraries that have open clubs. I typed in "online book clubs" and also got plenty of results. A third option is to ask friends and acquaintances at work or at your kids' school. Are they in book clubs? Are there openings for newcomers?

Choose a few communities to compare and contrast. Book clubs may not have websites or recorded events to peruse, but other types of communities will. Check them out. Then show up.

I suggest a *minimum* of three visits to each community, plus a meeting with the leader, if there is one, before making a decision about whether to join. If the leader cannot or will not meet with you, that might tell you something about how involved they are with individual community members, which may matter to you. Finding a community should feel like dating, with all of its frustrations, embarrassments, annoyances, relationship imbalances, and beautiful surprises. Your mantra is: *This takes work.*

Be curious. Take risks. Have patience.

Entering a room where you don't know the people or culture may feel like a risk. There are far too many communities in which members are not as welcoming to outsiders as one would hope, or as the members believe themselves to be. Even if it is your second or third visit, you are still an outsider, especially if the community has been meeting for quite a while. If you are an introvert, entering a new space will require outsize energy. If you are someone who has felt left out at other points in your life, you may be triggered. People who have been part of the community may know more about the topic than you do; you'll need to be open to learning and growth.

You might need to set a practical or emotional *kavanah*, an intention for showing up. A kavanah can be: "I will set a timer and only stay thirty minutes the first time I go," or "I have done harder things than this before, such as _____." I don't know you, but I do know that you can do this.

My suggestion on this last point is to hold some part of this initial experience in reserve for when you are an insider in a community. It may help you be more welcoming to all the newcomers who come after you.

Get involved.

If you find a place you think you can accept and where you will be accepted, wonderful! Now comes the second stage of dating: ascertaining if you're actually a match. Get involved. You cannot determine whether someone is a life partner without investing in the relationship. You cannot determine whether a community is worth your time without getting involved in the work.

Invite a few members of the community out for coffee, one-on-one. Hear their stories; tell them yours. Attend gatherings and meetings, and frequent their hangouts. Volunteer to make food or join a committee. This will not be easy. At times you may feel left out or a step behind everyone else. In those moments, remember that the work of being involved in community is so important that every Saturday morning at Jewish prayer services we say a special blessing for those people who "occupy themselves with the needs of the community."[42] As a show of how difficult this work is, note that we say this prayer when we are praying for world peace, which also requires many lifetimes of work!

Show up.

As a rabbi, I lead many multiweek classes, including workshops for interfaith couples, long-term introduction-to-Judaism workshops, or conversations across political differences. One of my primary goals in each of these cohorts is to build community, a sense of relationship and responsibility among participants. In order for that to happen, I have one simple requirement: People have to show up. If someone misses more than 20 percent of the classes, they are asked to step down and try again the next time one of these cohorts forms.

There is no malice in this rule. Participants have stepped down from classes for many good reasons, including sick parents or child care, or an intense time at work. When the goal is building a resilient and connected community, however, I am uncompromising. We cannot care for each other in the difficult moments if we do not show up and get to know each other in the mundane ones.

People who invest deeply in Jewish community can easily end up spending a half dozen hours a week caring for others, attending services, hosting holiday dinners, setting and changing communal policy, and attending each other's life-cycle events. Sometimes people do these things for their own benefit and sometimes it's for the good of the community or out of a sense of habit. Each of these reasons has one thing in common: It requires showing up. The only way people can get to know each other is by being in the same space alongside each other, otherwise, it can be too easy to make assumptions about people we have never met.

Spend time in real life with others in the community. Donate your time for volunteer efforts. When someone has a baby or a family member dies, bring the family food, if that is what they need. Watch out for the voices in your head that may mislead you by saying that there is someone else who can do whatever it is your community needs. You may be that person, and you can rarely go wrong by showing up.

Advocate to be better.

Once you are a part of the community, you will undoubtedly start to see some of its flaws. Perhaps people gossip too much, or the meeting space is not accessible to those with disabilities. Classes may be too pedantic or too traditional. Every community has its problems. Believing that your community must be perfect is naive at best, and dangerous at worst.

It is part of your responsibility as a community member to invest in the community's growth and success. When you notice something that you think should be changed, feel free to talk to different stakeholders and decision makers. Keep in mind that community change can take a very, very long time. Stick around, stay engaged, and make the effort.

As you get more involved, however, you may find that this community refuses to change. Please, give it as much time and effort as you can. At some point, however, it may be time to leave that group and start again.

On the other hand, perhaps helping build and make change in your community is what gives you a burgeoning sense of "home," a safe space in which you can be seen as your full self, with people you trust.

Build (if necessary).

If you cannot find a community after a lot of trying, build your own. Gather a small group of people who share a common interest. Ask each person to bring a plus-one so that there will be some diversity. Create goals, assign roles, and plan a calendar of gatherings. This, too, will be hard work.

I wish there were some short-hand way to build and maintain community, but that's just not the case. The process will be exhausting and exhilarating at the same time. When you feel dispirited, perhaps you can keep in mind that the work you do will benefit not only yourself, but also many people you do not even know yet.

Here are a few more words to the wise about community.

Communities have boundaries.

When you walk through many traditional Jewish neighborhoods, you may notice, strung from tree to tree or pole to pole, thin strings or wires pieced together to form a whole. This contraption is called an *eruv*. Inside the boundaries of the eruv, Jews may push strollers or walkers or carry bags or other goods on Shabbat. Without an eruv, which turns an entire neighborhood into one "home," Jews would not be permitted to carry or push anything outdoors.

Jews who observe the laws of the eruv do not think of it as magic. We understand that there is no actual difference between what happens within and outside the boundary. We have chosen a legal fiction, a human-created boundary within which a community functions. The eruv also represents an important Jewish teaching about what it takes to be a community—some people are in, and some are not.

All communities have boundaries, especially the closer you get to the core. A Democratic committee would not accept a Republican as a voting member. A community of bike riders would not allow on their trips someone who hates exercise. Some communities stop taking members once they reach a certain number of participants. Using the example of the book group, someone who hates reading and never reads the book should most likely be counseled out of the group.

This is not an argument for exclusion. Communities should open their doors as wide as possible, welcoming anyone who fits the community's requirements. Communities should also be free to keep out those who do not. A community of Black families, for instance, whose goal is to celebrate Black culture and explore the Black experience with people who share that experience, has the right to exclude families with no Black members. If a community requires people to attend a majority of its meetings in order to participate, then the group has the right to exclude people who do not abide.

A sixteenth-century rabbi argued that boundaried communities are good not only for the people who are inside them but for those who are on the outside.[43] When people are connected to others who share similar life experiences or goals and when they feel seen and cared for, they are happier. Happier people are more generous and physically healthy. They are almost certainly less lonely.

Radical welcoming

Even as I make an argument for boundaries, I will simultaneously make a full-throated plea for keeping the tent flaps of our community open as wide as possible. When Lisa and her fiancé stood before their community to be married, they were under a *chuppah*, the canopy under which a couple stands at a Jewish wedding. The chuppah, which is covered on top but open on all four sides, symbolizes the home the couple will build—one that is open and welcoming.

The Hebrew word *knesset* means assembly. (The Knesset most people are familiar with is the Israeli unicameral parliament.) A *beit knesset* is a house of assembly, or synagogue. Knesset also means "to welcome in." Judaism teaches that our synagogues are meant to be places of welcoming, not of exclusion. They are supposed to have windows so that congregants can see the world outside.[44] Our study halls, too, welcome people from far and wide.[45] The covenant that any community builds should be for the greatest number of people possible.[46]

If we want to create a community that is open, we will, at times, be in spaces with people whose ideas are different from ours and therefore deeply unsettling to us. Instead of writing those folks out of the community, I beg you to welcome them wherever possible, with compassion and empathy. Stay in conversation with *anyone* who is willing to engage with thoughtfulness, reflection, and integrity. Turn away only those who engage with hate, close-mindedness, or knee-jerk assertions that their way is the only way.

Community in action

Being in a community can both give you support and solace and be frustrating and enervating. But it's worth it. You deserve people who can pick you up when you are down, celebrate with you when you are joyful, and help you be resilient when times are tough. You deserve to be around people who let you know that you belong.

Chapter 8

The Way of *Tzedek*: Justice

Passover, which Jews have celebrated in some way for about three thousand years, is also known as the "Springtime Festival" and the "Holiday of Our Liberation." On Passover, we are commanded to remember our foundational story: We were slaves in Egypt long ago. And it is our task to fight for liberation for all those who do not yet experience it.

At the seder, we enter into a sort of willing fiction. In the *haggadah*, the book we read at the seder, it says, "In every generation, a human being is obligated to see themselves as if they were enslaved in Egypt."[1] Even as many of us sit in freedom around tables laden with food, we are tasked with feeling as if we ourselves were enslaved. The gambit is transparent: If we feel like we were enslaved but then freed, then it should inspire us to work for freedom for others around the world who remain subjugated. We imagine ourselves enslaved as an encouragement to do the work of *tzedek*, or justice, today.

Like many of the Hebrew words used in this book, tzedek contains layers. In ancient and medieval literature, it is most often connected to any type of just or reliable legal system. It can also mean "more correct in an ethical dilemma."[2] Sometimes, "tzedek" is used more like the English word "equity": a decision that is more generous to one party than another so as to make adjustments to previous imbalances.[3] It can also mean "honest," "true," or "fair."[4]

Tzedek is also about knowing when to compromise. An ancient story teaches of two boats encountering each other on a narrow river. If they attempt to pass each other at the same time, both will sink, as the river is not wide enough. But if they pass one after the other, they will both be safe. Similarly, the story tells of two camels who attempt to ascend a narrow, steep path at the same time. One camel must go behind the other, or they will both fall off the cliff.[5] In these cases, "tzedek" is defined as the boat captain who pulls to the side so the other boat can pass, or the camel driver who lets his camel go second.

No matter which definition you prefer, tzedek indicates a posture of empowered world changing. Our ancient texts teach that a *tzadik*—a person who practices tzedek—is the *yesod*, or foundation, of the world.[6] And as any contractor can tell you, a rotten foundation can take down a whole house.

In mystical terms, yesod means more than just foundation. It is what happens when inspiration and determination meet; it is action.[7] Tzedek is active. We pursue justice with the same intensity as we would an intruder who had broken into our home with the intent to kill us and our children.[8] We are told to refuse to let fear win. We must experience the same sense of urgency that we would if we learned that our house was about to fall apart with us in it, because that's what a world without justice represents.

Prophets versus rabbis

There are two basic models of tzedek. The first is the way of the prophet, who stands in the streets and proclaims loudly that change must happen. The prophet Isaiah furiously preached to the Israelites to feed the hungry, clothe the naked, house the poor, and not ignore the suffering of the needy.[9] Jeremiah urged the Israelites to help free people from oppressors, and to refuse to use violence against an immigrant or needy person.[10]

Prophets are often hated—especially while they are alive and prophesying.[11] This was as true in ancient times as it is today. In 2023, Dr. Martin Luther King Jr. had a 94 percent approval rating among Americans; at the time of his death, in 1968, he had a 33 percent approval rating. Rabbi Abraham Joshua Heschel, one of the most important rabbis of the twentieth century, wrote beautifully about why this might be. "The prophet," he writes, "hates the approximate; he shuns the middle of the road. . . . The prophet is strange, one-sided, an unbearable extremist."[12] Prophets understand that their words will alienate and infuriate many, but since they believe they are holding immutable truths, it doesn't bother them.

You, too, may believe so strongly in a cause that you are prepared to isolate yourself from loved ones with whom you disagree, to stand on street corners yelling through a megaphone at passersby, or ranting on the internet. You may not notice when you are hated. You may be doxxed and trolled. If you believe that your message is consequential enough, you may not care.

But take note: The ancient prophets were usually powerless and often ignored. The vast majority of prophets' prophecies came true dozens or hundreds of years after they lived, if at all. For that reason, some devalue the prophetic voice.

Judaism holds that the last of our "official" prophets died more than 2,300 years ago.[13] Today we might understand that some people carry a prophetic voice, or that they speak a certain kind of truth that is ahead of their time, or that they are exceedingly eloquent and relevant but are not meant to be taken literally as prophets.

In contemporary times, we believe that humans should not be deified, because that is a type of idol worship; it gives one individual human too much power. There is no one individual who understands what is right for the entire world. Too often, those who see themselves as contemporary prophets embody hubris and narcissism, the diametric opposite of prophecy. They are destructive, yelling that they know the one true way forward; they accuse others but do not look at themselves. Beware of those self-proclaimed prophets.

Some of us also critique the prophetic voice by saying that it is too idealistic and that it argues for the unachievable. Why keep talking about it? It's better to turn from the ideal to the achievable. If we focus too much on the impossible, we may miss critical wins and never achieve anything great.

I choose to see the prophetic voice as a north star. And just as I do not expect to reach the literal stars during my lifetime, I, too, will not bring about the entirety of the prophetic vision, no matter whose it is. But I know in what direction I should be heading.

The second model for pursuing tzedek is that of the ancient rabbis, who were *not* idealistic in their approach. Instead, they were quite systematic and practical. Consider the economic rules they proposed: In the prophetic imagination, people would just naturally share resources. In the rabbinic world, however, filled with people who are selfish or just self-centered, there are thousands of laws that create roadmaps to help us figure out how to build a more just and equitable world. Our rabbinic texts do not just say "clothe the naked" or "feed the needy" like the prophets did; they teach us *how* to establish a communal fund for the poor, or which specific workers' rights we must grant to those in our employ. The rabbis share the prophets' clear orientation toward a more just world, but with a much more practical bent.

Today, while we need to be very careful of anyone claiming the absolute clarity of a prophet, we should be careful not to suffocate prophetic voices. We need both prophetic and rabbinic voices in movements toward justice. Those who envision the ideal may refuse to be satisfied with less, but they will nonetheless "bend the arc of the moral universe toward justice," in the words of Theodore

Parker, an abolitionist minister. So, too, with those who work to alleviate suffering immediately and in this generation, one starfish at a time.

What does it look like to "pursue justice"?

The work of justice can be exhilarating, tedious, or infuriating. It can also be violent. Wars have been fought in pursuit of justice. People (including this person) have been arrested and tear-gassed at sit-ins. Close relationships have broken down and morphed into hatred. All of this prompts the question: How do we know when aggression is warranted or necessary in the pursuit of justice? This is one of the most difficult questions human beings can ask, because "justice" is defined differently by different people. Even when people *do* agree on the terms of justice, they may still disagree on the way to realize it.

In many cases, bringing justice to one group helps other marginalized communities. Recall what happened when the 1965 Voting Rights Act passed, allowing not only more Black Americans, but more Americans of every race, the right to vote. It is also true, however, that sometimes pursuing justice for one group comes at the expense of another, as in the case of civilian casualties during war. When it comes to justice, competing values often bump up against each other.

Sometimes I feel so confused and frustrated by questions like these that I'm inclined to step down from the work of justice altogether. I know that in a truly just world there would be no war, but there is no clear-cut agreement on how to get there. With this struggle in mind, I have attempted to put together some Jewish "must-haves" for the pursuit of justice.

A Jewish pursuit of justice does the following.

1. **Centers the good of society over an individual good.** Acts of tzedek are sometimes confused with acts of chesed. These two Jewish values overlap, but chesed is deeply connected to interpersonal relationships, and tzedek is more systemic in nature.

   Chesed is a voluntary act of kindness to another person, often someone you know or who is in your community. When you do chesed, it feels good because you immediately see the reward for your actions. The work of tzedek is about making changes that not only benefit individuals but also change systems.

2. **Is in service of the active and ongoing pursuit of peace.** A rabbi named Muna once taught that justice, truth, and peace are all the same. Peace cannot happen without justice, nor justice without peace.[14] In my justice work, especially if I am going to protest or disrupt, peace is my focal point. This teaching has been especially important to me when people I consider my allies in a social justice fight take up a new cause and invite me to join them. Instead of reflexively joining, Rabbi Muna teaches us to first study the cause. Do I actually believe this new strategy will bring us closer to peace, or do I just want to support people with whom I have worked in the past? If the answer is the latter, I need to work on staying in relationship with the allies but lovingly and clearly step back from this immediate cause.

3. **Is based on facts, not hearsay or half-truths.** We live in an
    empowered moment; the potential to search the internet for
    the widest range of facts is at our fingertips. We also live at
    quite a dangerous moment, for both falsehoods and facts
    are equally available, and we may not know the difference.
    If we are to pursue justice—and we should!—it must not
    be at the expense of truth. It benefits us to read widely and
    diversely, and to question what we learn.

4. **Demands compassion not only for your allies but also for
    your adversaries.** Dozens of years of working in different
    social justice movements have taught me that condescending
    to, demonizing, or dehumanizing my opponents makes me
    feel really good about myself for a moment. It also does not
    help the cause. Having compassion for other human beings
    does not mean that you must accept their points of view.
    It does not mean that you must forgive them their errors
    or missteps, especially if they don't take responsibility for
    them. In recognizing the humanity of the other, you, in
    your justice work, may be slightly less vindictive and more
    strategic. Compassion may also help you realize the ways
    you and your opponent are alike. All of the above can help
    you behave more morally and ethically—and do a better job
    of advancing your cause.

      Every human, from the kindest to the most evil, was
    created in the image of God. Whenever possible, we should
    flex our compassion muscles to include not just those with
    whom we agree but also those whose actions and even
    whose opinions we despise. If we cannot feel compassion
    for those with whom we disagree, then perhaps we can

have some for their descendants. Our texts tell the tales of descendants of three ancient leaders who did terrible things to the Israelite people: General Sisera, King Sennacherib, and King Nebuchadnezzar. From each of them, the texts teach, descended a number of righteous people, including two, Shamaya and Avtalyon, who were themselves leaders of the Jewish people. Even among the descendants of the evil Haman, who plotted to kill all the Jews, there were scholars of Judaism.[15]

These rabbinic texts are an attempt to create the world as the ancient rabbis wished to build it. The rabbis worked hard to imagine a way to find compassion for some of the people who have done the most evil in their world: Even if we cannot muster compassion for our direct adversaries, we can think of their children. Maybe their children will be different.

Admittedly, flexing our compassion muscles can be difficult, but we should still try. Gloating over an enemy's loss can get in the way of the pursuit of justice, for it takes our eyes off the prize, which is peace.[16]

5. **Is done as part of a community.** From almost the moment the Israelites left slavery in Egypt, God and the Israelite leadership understood that for this people to survive and thrive, they would need to grow from being a rag-tag group of individuals into a community of interdependence dedicated to a larger, unified cause. The first community center, then, was the "big tent" of the Mishkan, the tabernacle that the Israelites took from place to place while traveling from Egypt to the Promised Land. Working in community—or coalition, which is an oft-used term in the

justice world—keeps us from group-think or from assigning too much power to any one person. It exponentially increases the number of people who care about the issue at hand and who can therefore make a change by acting in concert.

Who is responsible for the work of justice?

Lest you think that the work of "justice" is only for marginalized groups, Judaism teaches us that it's critical for everyone. A better world for some is a better world for all, and it is the responsibility of all. We know this from a story about a cow.

The village was abuzz. It was Shabbat, and yet again Rabbi Elazar Ben Azarya's cow was walking around the village, a strap attached to its horns. Sunday through Friday, the strap was used to guide and direct the cow so it could give its milk and otherwise be led. But community law was that the strap should be removed for Shabbat, because on that day, everyone—including our farm animals—deserved a rest. So, Rabbi Elazar was in trouble for abusing his cow. Or wait—was he? There was a dispute.

Some townspeople pointed out that in general, Rabbi Elazar was a great guy who always gave to charity and cared for the community. And then it turned out that the cow in question belonged to Elazar's neighbor. Case closed. Elazar should be acquitted of all accusations.

But no. Because Elazar never said anything to his neighbor about how hard and inappropriately he was working the cow, it turns out that Elazar was still complicit in animal abuse. The moral of the story, according to the ancient rabbis, is that anyone who has the capability to protest the sinful conduct of the members of his household and does not protest is responsible for the sins of the members of his town.

The rabbis continue: If one is in a position to protest the sinful conduct of the people of their town and fail to do so, they are responsible for the sins of the people of their town. If one is in a position to protest the sinful conduct of the whole world and fail to do so, they are responsible for the sins of the whole world.[17]

In Judaism, inaction is a type of complicity. Part of the work of tzedek involves calling out injustice when we see it, whether in our own homes or on the street. This is not always easy, nor does it make you universally beloved. Many Jews throughout history have been imprisoned or even murdered because they took it upon themselves to protest injustice when they could have just stayed home.

Each of us is required to participate in the work of tzedek. In the words of the nineteenth-century poet Emma Lazarus, "Until we are all free, we are none of us free."[18] Hatred of one people often means hatred of another. I have the responsibility to fight not only for Jewish lives but also for those of other marginalized or oppressed populations.

Working for justice can be complicated. Research has shown that people who have experienced trauma have less capacity for empathy than those who have not.[19] I have seen that research manifested in many people I know; they feel like they don't have the capacity to work for liberation for anyone but the people they consider "their own." Even those who *intellectually* understand the ways that different oppressions intersect will sometimes turn a cold shoulder to others in need while taking care of their own. Ancient Jewish texts intuited that this would be the case, and they remind us over and over again that it is precisely *because* our ancestors experienced the trauma of slavery, and we experienced the discombobulation of being strangers, that we should care and work toward liberation for all—Jews and others—who remain subjugated. Our texts and teachings remind us that any one of us can participate in the oppression of others, even those of us who have experienced oppression ourselves.

Tikkun olam

The Hebrew phrase *tikkun olam*, "healing the world," has recently become well known, even beyond Jewish circles. More than one U.S. president has used it in his speeches. People young and old are attracted to this core Jewish value—that the world is broken (or at the very least, cracked), and it is our job to work to fix it. We don't hand over this world to any higher power or even any other person. Tikkun olam is upon each of us.

The work of pursuing equality, equity, and fairness is often lumped under the term tikkun olam. This phrase, which literally means "straighten" or "fix" the world, is, at its origin, a legal term. Scholars don't understand precisely what it means, but they do know that in its original iteration, the term was used to indicate a type of ruling that would keep the community running as smoothly as possible. The closer we get to a world in which people are treated equally, the smoother our world will run.

Is civic engagement the core of tzedek?

A story is told of a rabbi named Ami who was lying on his deathbed weeping when he received a visit from his sister's son. The nephew looked at his uncle with surprise. "Uncle, why are you crying?" he asked. "You are one of the most brilliant students and teachers of law in this generation. At this very moment, your students are sitting in your presence. You have done everything a person can do!" The nephew continued, in what feels like a non sequitur, "As an aside, I'm especially impressed that you spent your life studying Jewish text, and refrained from getting involved in the political morass of becoming a judge and overseeing the needs of the community."

Rabbi Ami told his nephew to stop talking. "My son," he said, "that is *exactly* why I am weeping! When I die and go to the world to come, I am worried that I will have to account for *refusing* to act as a judge. By separating myself from the community, I have abdicated my responsibility."[20]

Whatever newsfeed you read, watch, or listen to, one thing is clear: The American political system is in rough shape. There is a reason the word "politicking" has negative connotations. Even the truly idealistic can become cynical when watching the grandstanding, self-aggrandizement, and outright lying by people who were appointed or elected to serve.

When we bear witness to the worst of the political system, we may be inclined to overlook the best of it. I am proud of the American system of democracy, one that attempts to follow the will of the majority while protecting the rights of the minority. In the words of Winston Churchill, quoting an anonymous source, "Democracy is the worst form of government, except for all those other forms that have been tried."

Democracy did not exist as a concept for much of Jewish history, so one cannot say that democracy itself is a core Jewish value. One can, however, easily conclude that Jews are in favor of having a voice in their government. Ancient texts teach that it is optimal for people to choose their own leaders. Later on, once Jews entered democratic countries and were given the right to vote, they embraced that right with gusto. As Rabbi Moshe Feinstein wrote in 1984, "A fundamental principle of Judaism is . . . recognizing benefits afforded us and giving expression to our appreciation. Therefore, it is incumbent upon each Jewish citizen to participate in the democratic system which guards the freedoms we enjoy. The most fundamental responsibility of each individual is to register and to vote."[21]

In Rabbi Ami's rebuke, he reminded his nephew that participating in the process of governing is equally important to studying in the academy, if not more so. Rabbi Ami's argument was partially based on the often-cited understanding of the word "tzedek" in ancient times: the creation and implementation of a fair court system.[22] In this understanding of the word, tzedek happens when prosecutors who believe they have caught their criminal then learn something new that may let the defendant go free and pursue this new clue anyway.[23] Tzedek also happens when a judge rules in favor of someone not because they are poor or rich, but based only on the facts at hand.[24] When there are enough judges to fairly hear all the court cases on the docket—and enough lawyers to properly represent the defendants—this, too, is tzedek. Courts are so essential that Maimonides once taught that judges who do their jobs excellently, even for one hour, have "fixed the world entirely."[25]

It is not just the judicial system that Jews take seriously in any earnest conversation about tzedek. Over the course of our history, Jews have been persecuted and maltreated by many governments. With this in mind, we can understand the power of ethical governance. When the government functions properly, protecting the minority, eschewing corruption, and valuing truth, we are taught to respond as full and active participants. When it does not, we are taught to work assiduously to make it better, both for ourselves and for others. "The law of the land is the law," is an oft-repeated instruction in rabbinic texts.[26]

The ancient prophet Jeremiah lived during a time in which Jews were in the diaspora—exiled from the land of Israel—under a government that was not friendly to them. Jeremiah nevertheless taught us that wherever we live, and whenever we can, we should "build homes, and dwell in them . . . get married and have children . . . and seek the peace of the city, [even the one to which you have been] carried away captive . . . for in its peace you shall have peace."[27]

Notice that Jeremiah is teaching that we should not only *submit* to the rules of the state; we should also *build* and *seek* peace. If this is true in a land to which we had been "carried away captive," how much more so should it be true in the United States, a land the majority of Jews entered of their own free will?

Think of a big fish, one text teaches; in order to survive, that fish will swallow a smaller one alive. The brutal law of nature is true of humans as well. Perhaps in a messianic world we will be able to live peacefully without the need for governmental supervision.[28] We live in the real world, however, not an imagined one. Ever since biblical times, we have been taught that we need to be supportive of the government so that we do not, in the words of one famous text from two thousand years ago, "eat each other alive."[29]

Being "supportive" can include protest. If the government behaves in unethical or immoral ways, you are not permitted to "follow the multitude to do evil."[30] Instead, protest is encouraged and even required. Remember what we learned from Elazar's neighbor's cow about our responsibility to speak up! Protest is patriotic, because it means that we believe our country can do better. A country that quashes protest is almost always unsafe for Jews or other marginalized populations.

Is the world too broken?

Doing the work of tzedek can be exhausting. Sometimes, I'm overwhelmed by it. Even if you agree with every word I've written about tzedek so far, we are now, as we say in Hebrew, *b'lachatz*, pressured. Many Jews—many humans in fact—are squeezed tightly by fear, real and threatened violence, historical trauma, and hatred. I truly believe we cannot think entirely rationally under these circumstances. I'm left wondering: What can we do differently in the future?

As I lean against the metaphorical ancient trees that are Jewish texts, I'm reminded that we are not only supposed to pursue *justice* with intensity and single-mindedness; we are supposed to pursue *peace* that way, as well. I wrote above, and Judaism teaches, that in order to have peace, there must be justice.[31] If we find ourselves pursuing only one and sidelining the other, we are heading in the wrong direction. When ideological purity around justice cannot get us to peace, sometimes it is time to compromise.[32]

About 1,200 years ago, a rabbi named Simon wove a tale about the creation of humanity. Before humans were created, God—and God's angels—were unsure about humanity. The angel named Chesed said, "Yes! Create them, because they will do good in the world." Truth argued against it, saying that humans would be "full of lies." Tzedek said, "Yes! They will do acts of justice." Peace said, "Nope, they'll just fight."[33] God knew that Truth and Peace were correct. God created human beings anyway.

Two verses from Deuteronomy emphasize this tension. One line reads: "There will be no poor among you,"[34] and just a few lines later another reads: "When there is a poor person in your midst" . . . when, not if. This is the paradox we have to live with. On the one hand, we strive for the prophetic world, in which there is no poverty. On the other, we live in the rabbinic world, in which poverty exists. It's our responsibility to set up systems to care for people in need.

We all have choices when it comes to tzedek. For instance, consider Moses, who grew up in Pharaoh's palace, perhaps even having Pharaoh's mindset. Moses also knew that he was from the nation of people who were enslaved. He escaped the palace and journeyed to the desert of Midian. He became a shepherd, lived with the family of Jethro, and learned a new set of values. Moses saw in a burning bush a vision of divinity, which told him that we must value not opulence or pyramids but instead the other, the human oppressed in our own backyard. Moses was told he had a responsibility to help the enslaved people, but he was reluctant. He had made a life for himself in Midian, had found a wife and a career. He was scared. Five times he declined the demand that he go back to Egypt and help bring justice. He was finally convinced when he was allowed to return with an ally, his brother, Aaron.

"Let my people go!" Moses demanded of Pharaoh, in the palace in which he grew up.[35] But Pharaoh's heart was hard.

Moses could have gone home at that point, back to Midian, where things were safe and quiet. He could have asked Pharaoh if he could come back to the palace, to resume his life as a prince. But Moses never let go of his goal of tzedek.

You are Moses. You have a choice. In the words of Rabbi Becky Jaye, "There are two dimensions to the risks we face. The first, of course, is the actual crisis at hand—climate change, racism, and so on. The second is our emotional and spiritual state in response. If we allow fear and despair to paralyze us, we lose all ability to respond to the crisis, which digs us deeper into a destructive cycle. But if, like this Pharaoh, we can move beyond the terror to seeking options with an open mind, we may find ourselves with more resources at hand than we ever realized was possible."

I hope that you choose to lift up the voices of chesed and tzedek and to engage with the world, do good, and work for justice.

One more thing: You, too, are Pharaoh. We each have at least a little bit of Pharaoh in us, the part of us that turns away, or believes lies because they are less painful than facts.

Those of us who have read the biblical story of the exodus from Egypt may know of the seven times that God hardened Pharaoh's heart. But did you know of the three times that Pharaoh hardened his own heart, without any involvement from God?[36]

Selfishness, greed, money, and hatred are not new. So, too, is living as if in a state of scarcity, even when we have a life of abundance. As in Pharaoh's palace, so today. Compassion toward the vulnerable is also eternal. Truth is eternal. We have a choice as to which values we will uphold.

Chapter 9

The Way of
Shabbat: Ceasing + Resting

Twenty-first-century technology and culture make constant demands on our attention. Our phones buzz with pop-ups. Netflix always has another show for us to binge. We can't even fill our car with gas or wait for a bus without a flashing advertisement. Even when we do have free time, some of us feel guilty for not generating value or being "useful."

"Busy-ness" is not only a twenty-first-century problem. For much of human history, it was expected that most people would work from sunup to sundown and then sleep until it was time to get up and work all over again. Modern inventions, like the washing machine and the internal combustion engine, added an ease and flexibility to our lives that our ancestors did not enjoy.

It is for all of these reasons and a few more that Shabbat is one of the most important religious (human?) innovations of all time. Few things are more critical than taking time (or better yet, feeling *required* to take time) to recharge from the pressures the world puts on us.

For thousands of years, Judaism has held that observing Shabbat—a prescribed day of "ceasing"—is a critical part of human flourishing. It is so important, in fact, that even God does it. After God created the world in six days, our biblical story goes, on day seven, God ceased from doing any work. Notice how important creativity is here. For six days, God creates. Notice also how important not-creating is.[1] On Shabbat, we imitate God's rest; we stop trying to shape the world, and instead are content simply to be in it.

The word "Shabbat" is often translated as "a day of rest," but the observance of Shabbat is less about hurkle-durkle (the ancient Scottish practice of lounging in bed) and more about removing ourselves from the workaday world. While there is overlap in these two concepts, they are not the same.

While Shabbat is not necessarily about ease or peace, those certainly factor in. Shabbat is about dwelling within the world, our communities, and ourselves without trying to change anything. It reminds us that being partners in creation necessitates our stepping back and taking time to reflect on that work. In traditional Jewish communities, Shabbat is observed for a full twenty-five hours, from sundown on Friday night until almost an hour after sundown on Saturday night.

Here are eight main Shabbat observances that, practiced weekly, can increase your connection to others as well as to yourself.

1 Sometimes we have to be a little quiet.

Traditional Shabbat practice includes three special meals. We may begin with a few prayers of gratitude, then eat delicious food, which in my home is almost always take-out. Shabbat dinner is on Friday night and Shabbat lunch is at midday on Saturday. *Seudah shlishit*, the third meal, is meant to fall an hour or two before the end of Shabbat, late on Saturday afternoon.

One college summer, a friend came to visit me at my parents' home. This woman was a talker; I'm sure you know the type. She was smart and had interesting things to say but didn't know when to stop.

The week of my friend's visit, my parents had also invited a couple of dear friends to Shabbat dinner. Two smart, interesting people. Unfortunately, they couldn't get a word in with my friend at the table. Well into the meal, one of my parents' friends leaned over, gently but firmly put her hand on my friend's arm, and said to her, "It's time to be quiet now." There was no malice, no aggression. Just this simple statement: "It's time to be quiet now."

Thirty years later, my husband, Russell, and I say this sentence to each other all the time. We, too, do it with neither malice nor aggression. He might come home from a long and tough day at work and I'll brightly say, "Tell me all about your day!" He replies, "It's time to be quiet now." I understand. He'll talk when he's ready. Maybe he needs to reflect on something. Maybe I'm taking up so much space that he can't find himself or process what he wants to say. Sometimes a little quiet is better than a lot of words.

Judaism interweaves body and spirit, future and past, happy and sad. The loud and the quiet are interwoven as well, although the quiet sometimes gets lost in the noise. Jewish culture actively *encourages* children to fight for their voices to be heard at the dinner table or in synagogue. Jewish "loud" holidays, such as Purim, on which we're commanded to party, or Passover, on which we gather around a table for a wine-fueled Socratic symposium, are some of our favorite "holy" times.

Likewise, in the United States, we are so focused on being heard—as individuals, as a people—that it's as if a few moments of quiet are anathema to our own sense of dignity. If we don't post about it, did it really happen? Everyone has an opinion about everything. While all of us want to be recognized and appreciated for who we are, many of us assume that what it takes to be seen is to be LOUD.

Shabbat teaches us that sometimes "it's time to be quiet now." Six days a week, the pressures and the pace keep us from reflecting and noticing. The Shabbat pace is slower and more reflective. Shabbat, at its best, is more interested in the give-and-take of deep conversation than in soliloquies or filibustering. Out of the quiet, new insights arise.

Slowing down is not always comfortable. Rabbi Kalonymus Kalman Shapira, the chief rabbi of the Warsaw ghetto during the Holocaust, teaches that when we *are* able to slow down, the first emotion we may notice is discomfort. He calls it "a tentative probing of the soul." I'd call it a surfacing of disparate thoughts and feelings that we might otherwise ignore. The discomfort may make us feel uneasy or irritated and may incline us to distract ourselves with food or drink or TV or computer games.

We will do quite a lot, Rabbi Shapira teaches, to divert attention from whatever pain or sadness we notice in the quiet. Instead, perhaps we should allow ourselves bandwidth to work through our feelings, which is almost always better than sublimating them and hoping that they go away. Spoiler alert: They do not.

When you peel away the distractions and just listen to the heart, soul, and *kishkes* (stuffed sausages, a Jewish food favorite, but it also means "guts")—whether you're talking about your loved ones or the direction of your own life—you may gain clarity; sometimes, you can find deep joy. At other times, all you can access is pain and sadness, which is hard, but not as difficult as pretending they don't exist. On Shabbat, we attempt to be in touch with these feelings. Rabbi Shapira wants to inspire us to "clearly, consistently, and diligently slow down and learn to observe." When we feel deeply, we become more "open and alive," which takes time, certainly more time than any one day of Shabbat. We have many stages to go through first—frustration, anger, boredom, even discerning basic truth—before we can process our most complicated feelings. Guess what? Shabbat comes every week.

Shabbat is a time to be quiet now, breathing more deeply, reading and allowing the mind to get distracted, taking long walks and playing board games with family. It's a time of not allowing the incessant drumbeats of daily life to distract us from what is in front of us.

To be quiet often requires a nudge from someone wise. This is where Judaism comes in. We have millennia of teachings and guidance about how and when to adopt that slower pace. We have laws that "require" us to quiet down on Shabbat, whether we like it or not. The strictest Shabbat practices include refraining from driving, using technology, spending money, writing, and more. Our "time to be quiet now" does not come spontaneously, and we do not need to fumble around to figure out what silence can look like. Judaism offers wisdom on all these pieces, big and small.

2 Time is even more sacred than things.

Sometimes I think that whoever wrote the old Mastercard commercials had spent time with Rabbi Abraham Joshua Heschel. "Dinner out with family: $250. Time together: priceless." I don't know how Rabbi Heschel, a social justice activist, textual scholar, and philosopher, would have felt about the first half of the advertisement, but he would have agreed with the latter half. Heschel was a fierce advocate for the immeasurable worth of time, using Shabbat as his prime example. He reminded us of the fact that every hour is "the only one given at the moment, exclusive, and endlessly precious."[2] Heschel taught that one of Judaism's core principles is to learn how to elevate many of these unique hours from the banal to the sacred. We cannot make every single hour of every single day holy, but we can make one day a week (Shabbat) pure holiness. The hours of Shabbat, Heschel teaches, are Judaism's "great cathedrals."[3]

We each have an unknown number of hours on this Earth. Every hour, every moment, is sacred, even if they cannot all be used for sacred purposes. Marking Shabbat every single week forces us to recognize the preciousness and precariousness of each moment. A temple can be destroyed, a trinket lost, but you can take Shabbat with you wherever you go. This is an especially poignant teaching for the Jews, a people who have been forced out of so many homes and a homeland and robbed of so many physical possessions over history.

In the late 1990s, my husband and I spent a year traveling around the world, visiting fifteen countries. From Thailand to Cambodia to Ecuador, no matter where we were each week, we would celebrate Shabbat. In Bali, we marked Shabbat outdoors and poolside, surrounded by lush vegetation, more orchids than one could count, and our new English friends, Miranda and Jackie, who taught us yoga and meditation. In Nepal, we had Shabbat in a makeshift sukkah built by Israelis who also were traveling the world and who had bought saris in Kathmandu and wood from along the Annapurna Circuit trails to build the hut in which we celebrated the holiday. (For the fall holiday of Sukkot, Jews build temporary outdoor huts, roofed with natural materials like branches or bamboo. They are often decorated with paper chains, fairy lights, and other fun decorations, and when it is not raining, we eat festive meals inside them. Some Jews even sleep outside in their sukkot!) We had dinner in Havana with some of the few hundred Jewish residents left in Cuba, people who generously shared their scarce resources with us. There were no cathedrals; there was only Shabbat.

Shabbat happens every single week, Friday evening to Saturday night, whether we observe it or not. There is no Jewish tradition of marking Shabbat on Tuesday rather than Saturday because, for instance, Tuesday may be more practical for one family member or another. Part of the magic of sacred time is that you are not marking it alone. Millions of people across the globe are experiencing that special Shabbat energy; your moment of ceasing is being shared with people in Peru, Vietnam, and West Virginia. This energy is best evidenced in cities like Jerusalem or neighborhoods where the preponderance of people mark sacred time in the same way.

The rabbis often talk about Shabbat personified as a queen or a bride. She is there every week, but we are in control of how we interact with her. We can open the door and invite her into our lives. Sometimes we will be able to be in the relationship for the full twenty-five hours, and sometimes we will be lucky to get in an hour.

We do not have to create Shabbat from scratch: The turning of the planet and the setting of the sun is what makes it Shabbat. This feels like a relief. The image of Shabbat standing on our doorstep can also seem like a burden. At whatever point you are able to plug in to Shabbat, know that it will be available to you. There is no pressure. Shabbat is patient.

3 We are more than what we earn.

I live in Washington, DC, a city where the first question many people ask upon meeting someone new is, "What do you do?" People are not just proud of their work; they are often boastful. They compete for professional influence or income. They live to work.

It is obvious to me why many Washingtonians need a Shabbat. Even for those who work to live (and not the other way around), a job can sometimes get in the way of a life. Almost half of American workers don't take all the vacation time that is allotted to them.[4] The gig economy, in which people piece together hourly work, and the fact that workers are often not even told *when* they will be working until a day or two before their shift, creates a hustle culture where parents are forced to choose overtime over family time, and in which there is less of a boundary between work and home. Human dignity is diminished when humans are treated as cogs in a piece of machinery rather than as individuals who are more than the servants of their masters, even if they are well paid.

Shabbat comes to teach us that we are more than our jobs and that we should aspire to the goal that ceasing-from-work is a human right. For those of us who are not our own bosses (and even for some of us who are), society needs to provide scaffolding and structures that encourage or even force us to stop working. Whether that is paid vacation, a supervisor who respects that you choose not to answer emails on the weekend, a work schedule supplied weeks in advance, or the broader protections of labor unions, rest does not exist in a vacuum. A Shabbat discipline acknowledges this reality and incites the world around us to change.

Over two thousand years ago, the rabbis created a fixed system for how to cease from the creative labor of the rest of the week. They developed a system of thirty-nine "labors" that are forbidden on Shabbat.[5] Obviously, nowhere in ancient texts does it say, "Do not answer work emails on Shabbat." Instead, some of the actions forbidden are weaving, cooking, tanning hides, and writing—in other words, actions that lead to the creation of something new. Those who adhere strictly to Shabbat rules and regulations do not write in a journal, knit, or bake cookies on Shabbat, even though refraining from these actions can feel at odds with our sense of what is restful and nourishing. On Shabbat, we cease from *creative labor*, that which changes the world in some way.

Refraining from "labor" doesn't mean we cannot do anything difficult. For example, hosting a Shabbat lunch for a dozen people is entirely acceptable, and we can all agree that this is not easy! The concept of "labor" can still guide us. What are the firm boundaries we need so that this day, Shabbat, does not feel like all the other days? What is the discipline we need for rest to be nourishing?

The Ten Commandments are well known as some of the most important rules in the Jewish tradition. They appear twice in the Bible and include a commandment to honor Shabbat—but with a slight difference each time. In the first mention, the Israelites are commanded to "*remember* the Shabbat day and keep it holy," using the Hebrew word *zachor*.[6] In the second, the command is to "*guard* the Shabbat day and keep it holy," using the Hebrew word *shamor*.[7] The rabbis notice this difference and interpret "remember" and "guard" as embracing two different facets of Shabbat. "Guard," they teach, refers to all the things we do *not* do on Shabbat—the "labor" we discussed earlier. "Remember," on the other hand, refers to all the things we *do* on the Shabbat, all the active steps we take to make Shabbat holy and special. "Guard" refers to the *don'ts*, "remember" to the *dos*.[8]

"Guard" and "remember" teach that resting from creation, stepping away from always needing to *add* to the world, can take different forms. This is borne out by research. We need many kinds of rest.[9] We can understand shamor, "to guard," as encouraging us to attend to our need for passive rest. Shamor is about NOT doing. This is what likely first comes to mind when you imagine "rest." Shamor is spending a day in your pajamas on the couch, or languorous hours with a novel. Shamor is the out-of-office message, the saying NO to one more commitment. With "guard" types of rest, we protect ourselves. We keep our weary souls from the cacophony of the world and its demands; we put up boundaries and carve out quiet time; we seek peace.

The kind of rest characterized by "remember" is different. Zachor is about resting actively, the rest that we might have to push ourselves to do. This is the rest of an afternoon exploring an art museum, of a stroll through the park or a hike in the woods. This is the rest we find when we spend time with loved ones or people we are just getting to know. This is the rest we find in prayer or meditation, whether we seek out that spiritual time alone or in community. "Remember" is about, well, remembering. When we rest actively, we remember who we are: what is important to us and what our values are. The rest we find in "remember" is about clearing away the noise to return to the activities, people, and communities that are essential to our souls.

These examples of "remember" and "guard" are pretty individualistic. If we focus only on how we can rest as atomized, separate people, we miss the essence of Shabbat: rest for the whole world.[10]

Caring for ourselves inspires us to care for others.

At the beginning of Shabbat dinner on Friday night, we say a prayer over wine that includes a perhaps surprising line, which I will paraphrase: We are grateful for Shabbat because it is a reminder of the fact that the Jews were enslaved in Egypt thousands of years ago, and were then freed.

Some rabbis ask: What does the ancient story of enslaved Israelites have to do with our celebration of Shabbat today? Even on our day of ceasing-from-creating, we are meant to remember that the Jewish foundational story is that we were slaves, then we were freed, and now it is our responsibility to work for freedom for all people. This day of rest for ourselves and our inner circles is meant to inspire us to use the other six days of the week to work for people who do not have the same choice.

The biblical commandment to observe Shabbat does not just apply to you, the individual. The text teaches that "you shall not do any work—you, your son or your daughter, your male or female laborers, your ox or your ass, or any of your cattle, or the stranger in your settlements, so that your laborers may rest as you do."[11] Shabbat is not just about each of us resting in our own little bubble. It is about a *vision* of rest (both active and passive) that extends to everyone with whom we interact, as well as those in even wider circles.

Some people proudly argue that Shabbat is the impetus for the concept of a "weekend." I do not know if that is factually true, but what I do know is that many Jews were among the labor and union activists that fought for many kinds of workers to have weekends off. It was not that the bosses had a moral dedication to enabling rest among their workers—often just the opposite. Employees had to band together to achieve this right.[12] Part of building a world that includes Shabbat is creating one that inspires us to continue to expand the circles of ceasing so that people in all parts of society gain the right to rest and reflect and do not need to work themselves to absolute exhaustion in order to survive.

5 Nonstop consumerism makes us less happy, not more so.

When we consider what makes Shabbat a day when we can rest on our own and move the world toward rest, an essential element is our wallets. It is often through purchasing and spending that we draw on the labor of others. All the people involved in each transaction have the potential to be harmed by our spending choices.

Consider two experiments. In the first, college students were asked to complete questionnaires about photos of either luxury goods or scenes of nature. Those viewing the fancy cars, gadgets, and jewelry were more likely to say they felt sad or anxious than those who looked at the nature scenes. In another experiment, students were presented with a hypothetical water shortage and then asked to identify themselves as "consumers" or "individuals." People who identified as "consumers" were less trusting of others. They cared more about hoarding water for themselves than about solving the problem for everyone.[13]

Spending money should be a *tool* rather than an end in itself, yet it often ends up as the latter rather than the former.[14] Capitalism pushes us to want more stuff, when it is social bonds and experiences that make us happier. For some, consumption can become a type of addiction. Consumerism has been referred to as "an infectious disease"; being around other consumers makes us more likely to consume for the sake of consuming, and not because we actually have a need for the items we are purchasing.[15]

One way to break yourself of an addiction is to detox, to go "cold turkey," and separate yourself from other people who are part of the problem. On Shabbat, tradition teaches that we refrain from purchasing *anything*: no errands, no internet purchases, no restaurants. The wallet goes away for a full twenty-five hours.

When you remove yourself from the materialistic, consumerist world, you recognize quite quickly that many of us place too much emphasis on money and what it can buy, on the people who have it and the people who do not. When we cease purchasing even for just a few hours, we contribute to a more equal, less competitive world. You don't have to worry about your friends going to brunch at an expensive restaurant that you cannot afford, for instance, because you will not be going to *any* restaurant. You can invite people over for a simple meal instead.

When we cease from using money for a small period of time each week, we are forced to acknowledge the ways in which money is a crutch. Going shopping can sometimes be a way to run from, rather than toward, our loved ones and our own internal processing. Taking time to refrain from interacting with a materialistic economy forces us to pause and reflect instead.

Whether you abstain from using money for two hours a week or a full twenty-five, consider "money Shabbat" as a time to refrain from buying and selling. It will force you to develop all sorts of different muscles, such as those of just being with others, with no set agenda.

6 Friends do not let friends Shabbat alone.

All week long, many of us spend time around other humans. At work, on public transportation, or in the supermarket, we stand shoulder to shoulder with other people who fulfill our utilitarian needs. With these people, the Jewish philosopher Martin Buber teaches, we are in an "I–It" relationship; we see them as a means to an end. There is nothing inherently wrong with this type of relationship. We have to get through our days, and we all want to have our basic needs met and do what is necessary to make sure our loved ones' needs are also met.

These "I–It" relationships cannot satiate our bodies, minds, or souls. If the rest of the week is a "fast food" approach to relationships, Shabbat is "slow food." On Shabbat, we spend time with people, but in a different way. We build a covenantal community with like-minded people who also want to engage more deeply, thoughtfully, and meaningfully. When done well, Shabbat relationships move from being "I–It" to "I–Thou" and even beyond: They move from being expedient and functional to being holy, which in Judaism means "set apart."

Shabbat simultaneously invites us into a form of I–Thou relationship and inspires us to transcend the one-on-one to the holiness of the entire community. Jewish tradition holds that there are very few activities a person should do alone; that even includes Shabbat. One reason Shabbat works is that it is communal as well as personal. Traditionally, this has meant time spent in synagogue and around dining tables, praying and studying and singing together.

For those who are not Jewish or who are not interested in synagogue or prayer, there are many ways to create a Shabbat community.

- Have a supper club, a potluck dinner with rotating hosts.
- Get a group together for weekly board game night.
- Sing! Anything you want: Broadway tunes, folk music, whatever lights you up!
- Gather a walking or hiking group.

Shabbat groups don't have to be composed of people who all deeply love each other; that would make it a friendship group or—sometimes—a family. Shabbat groups might be composed of "accountability partners" who help us achieve our goals in life and make us our best selves. Spending time with humans you love or care for is a critical way to evade loneliness and its resulting increase in major diseases that can have an effect on public health as well as on individuals. It is also valuable to spend time with humans with whom you share a common goal—quieting down and listening more reflectively, or singing with gusto, or taking long walks in nature, or learning something new.

As we have noted, Shabbat is an opportunity to be by ourselves but also with the people and interests that bring us beyond ourselves. This requires spending time with close friends and family, and reaching out to widen our circles. The relationships that Shabbat engenders are those of deep one-on-one connection. They also lead us to become part of a community of common experience or purpose. Shabbat invites us to dive deeper into relationships we already hold dear, and to build new ones.

7 Unfettered technological access is addictive and therefore dangerous.

Americans spend more than five hours a day on their phones. That's only 1.5 hours less than the amount of time that the average American *sleeps* each night.[16] Using our phones can sometimes be helpful or lifesaving. Much of the time, though, we stare at them because we're addicted. Time slips away from us while we scroll through social media. We glance at a text while we are driving. We experience "phantom vibrations," when we think our phone is buzzing but it actually is not. It has been found that increased physical and mental health issues, including eye strain, neck pain, back pain, depression, loneliness, mood disorders, and sleep disturbances, can be attributed to the excessive use of smartphones. Even a small reduction in smartphone use—one hour per day—can make a difference, reducing depression and anxiety and improving physical activity.

For these reasons, every few years, the concept of a "tech Shabbat" has a resurgence: An op-ed in a popular newspaper or magazine makes a case for leaving our phones in a drawer for a day, setting an auto-response, and ignoring our emails. If I have not yet convinced you of the importance of getting away from our phones, try this: For the next few days, notice the ways in which you use technology, not only to make your life easier but also to create a barrier between you and other humans or the natural world. What would be different if you refrained from using technology for a full day? Would you look up while walking the dog and see a neighbor or a rainbow? Would you play with your child instead of taking videos or photos of them? Would you disengage from the dopamine highs and lows of social media? Would you walk into a room and look around for someone to talk to, rather than stare at your phone until someone talks to you?

The step after noticing is execution. On Shabbat, it's traditional to refrain from using not only your phone, but any sort of distracting technology. If you cannot abandon your phone or laptop completely—perhaps you are caring for a child or aging parent and must be reachable—consider taking steps to reduce the incessant pull of technology. Try changing your phone settings to select which notifications will buzz. You can choose accept messages and calls only from a defined list of people. Or change your screen to black-and-white to take the power away from the bright colors of Instagram. Delete or block social media apps so that you can only post from a computer or check updates at certain times. Can you try it for a day? Shabbat is an ideal time to cut back.

8 If we say we will have Shabbat "when we get to it," we will never get to it.

Any one of us who has ever learned a language, or trained for a race, or studied for a big end-of-year or certifying exam, understands the importance of discipline. You cannot just get up in the morning and decide to run a marathon. It takes time and patience.

The same is true of weekly Shabbat practice. Too many of us will find excuses *not* to observe Shabbat. It can feel near-impossible to establish that type of discipline. Research about habit formation is not new, nor is it surprising: It's hard; repetition is key; and it can take anywhere from 18 to 254 days to truly form a new habit.[17]

You have to start somewhere. On Shabbat, you create a window of opportunity to derail existing habits and create new intentions. Like most other difficult things worth doing, this happens in increments, by providing space where the small changes can take root. If we live our lives on a constant treadmill, we never give ourselves the opportunity to see what a different future could look like.

The generative, additive, and inspirational moments of vacation, the ones that are designed to galvanize us even after we've returned to our regular lives, happen on Shabbat when we force a pause and encounter a different reality. It takes the repetition of Shabbat after Shabbat, week after week, to make a lasting change. When we stop and see the world in a different way, even if only for a short while, we may be inspired to treat those other six days, that non-Shabbat time, a little bit differently as well.

Shabbat practice will take a major push of willpower to start. What begins as a habit that requires discipline can morph into a treat we look forward to, or a return to ourselves that we come to rely on. Give yourself the gift of Shabbat—put some energy into making Shabbat happen for you. Starting small can lead to a big change.

Chapter 10

The Way of
Aveilut: Mourning

When my dad went into remission after having lymphoma, we decided to have a party. It was held at a playground called Candy Cane City, where each year we spent Thanksgiving morning playing a football game we unoriginally titled the Turkey Bowl. My husband and I hosted a baseball game the weekend of our wedding at Candy Cane City. The place already had a lot of history for our family.

My dad's name was Ned, so the theme of the party was The Grateful Ned. We presented all the guests with baseball caps with that line, plus a red ribbon in honor of those fighting lymphoma. When my dad first started to lose his hair and people wanted to know how they could help, we asked them to send him hats. At the party, we decorated the backstop with over a hundred hats of all sorts that he had been given. Berets, baseball caps, ski caps, even one ushanka, a Russian fur hat with earflaps. The party was informal and filled with the laughter of lots of people who knew each other, including many who had cared for my father while he was ill. People came from all over to celebrate.

A few weeks after the party, my father's cancer came back. It was incurable. He died a year later.

In her book *Maybe You Should Talk to Someone*, the psychotherapist Lori Gottlieb writes about one of her patients, Julie, who finds out she has terminal cancer and asks, "Will you stay with me until I die?" Gottlieb writes, "And right then, the nature of our work together changed: I was going to help her come to terms with her death." They were both bereft, and they both accepted the reality laid out before them. That's the Jewish approach to death and dying in a nutshell. We are alive at this moment; we won't always be. In an hour, a month, a thousand months, we're going to die. We don't know when or how or why. And when we die, whatever age it is, it will be sad. While contemporary culture often encourages us to avert our eyes when confronting death, Judaism encourages us to face the reality of mortality and the sadness of loss after someone is gone.

Sitting with someone else in their sadness is one of the most difficult things we can do. Many of us want to make it all better, and we are wont to say such things as, "They are in a better place now." And while some of us may believe that is true, the best we have to offer when sitting with a mourning friend or family member is not platitudes but presence. Instead of "Everything happens for a reason," Jewish phrases of comfort include "May their memory be for a blessing," or "May you be comforted among all who mourn." We acknowledge the loss but also the truth that the mourner is profoundly un-alone. They have the memory of the person who died, they have the community of others who mourn, and they have you.

In traditional Judaism, the word "mourner" is a technical term, covering only the sibling, child, parent, or spouse of the deceased. On the one hand, I appreciate the acknowledgment that there *is* a difference in feeling in a "first degree" loss. On the other hand, "first degree" may feel different in the twenty-first century than in the first. For that reason, you may consider yourself a "mourner" if you lose a best friend, grandparent, in-law, or another person with whom you have been in a long-term, intimate relationship.[1]

Human beings (and some animals!) are creatures of ritual, especially around death.[2] When someone we love dies, ritual can take us through the immediate, crushing loss as well as through every stage of grief. It provides a set of steps in predetermined order so that we do not have the burden of creating a new structure during a tumultuous time. It offers the community a way to care for mourners during our time of more intense need. It also offers second- or third-degree mourners permission to mourn, even if we did not have as close a connection with the deceased as the primary mourners.

Ritual is critical, since right after a loved one dies, survivors are often numb, in shock, confused, or all of these. While this is especially true in the context of a sudden or tragic death, it can also be true after the long illness of an older person, who you may have grown to believe would live forever. Judaism has very specific, time-tested practices around death that happen whether or not it was a tragic death, and whether or not you have a busy week of work ahead of you. They happen regardless of whether you even liked the person who died.

In the Jewish tradition we bury our dead as soon as possible, sometimes within twenty-four to forty-eight hours. This period is called *aninut*, the "time of impoverishment." Note that it is a loss of a beloved human being, and not a loss of money, that makes us "poor." During this initial moment of trying to figure out a myriad of details, the deceased's loved ones are not even yet called "mourners," acknowledging that (a) feelings can be so intense that sadness has not fully set in, and (b) there is so much work to be done to prepare for the funeral and its surrounding events that loved ones do not have time to mourn appropriately. Mourners are encouraged—and often need—to entirely alter their patterns of living, including not doing any housework or professional work, and not engaging in any joyous activities such as attending parties or eating fancy meals. If you are in aninut, you are not expected to be a host, or even to welcome visitors into your home if you do not want them there. If anyone does come to your home, their job is to care for you, and not the reverse.

How can I mourn Jewishly if I can't even get time off from work?

While the majority of businesses offer bereavement leave, it is often unpaid or just a few days.[3] Given that 78 percent of people live paycheck to paycheck,[4] 24 percent have no paid vacation leave, and almost 10 percent of people who *do* have vacation days do not take them because they are afraid they will be fired, I can understand why it might feel imperative to continue working through a loss. (I will also comment here, however, that our tradition curses those who require people in mourning to work.[5])

If you are in mourning, ask if you can take time off. Your boss may be more empathetic than you think. But even if that's not the case, you may plant a seed in your boss's mind for the future. If you must work, then make sure your colleagues know about the loss. Talk to them about your loved one; keep a photo in your pocket. In Judaism, mourners tear a piece of their clothing (or a black ribbon that you pin to your clothing) and wear it for at least seven or up to thirty days after a death so that no one (including you!) can forget what you are going through at this moment.

One reason that aninut is so compressed and hectic is because directly after death, the most important value is maintaining respect and dignity for the deceased. The Hebrew term for this is *chesed shel emet*. It means selfless lovingkindness, the kind of mitzvah that is done without expectation of reciprocation. This is the way that, ideally, all mitzvot should be carried out. From the moment someone passes away until they are buried, the body is not left alone. (This is true for the final days of someone's life, as well.) To be perfectly honest, this tradition comes from an ancient time in which a body left alone would quickly be decimated by predatory animals.[6] (For those who want to follow this teaching, it may be comforting to know that being in a hospital morgue, which often is staffed by multiple people, counts as "protected status" for the body. An additional watchperson is not required.)

What is the contemporary meaning in this ancient tradition, especially for those of us who will not be burying our loved one within forty-eight hours? Our ancient rabbis thought that for three days after death, "the soul is hovering over its grave, believing that it will return."[7] Maybe that is true; maybe not. But what if we flip this teaching on its head? For the first three days after someone dies, what if it's not the *deceased's* soul that believes that it will return, but instead the *living* who are in disbelief?

If that is true, it can lead us to two meaningful conclusions. We accompany the dead so that (a) the fact can sink in that they are gone from this world, which helps us move from numbness to sadness, and (b) we can recognize that one day, we will also be gone from this world. This is a final lesson and a gift from the deceased. What will we do with our precious days left on Earth?

The funeral and burial

Many people take on debt to pay for a funeral.[8] Our tradition holds that it is better to spend money on the living than on the dead. There *are* Jewish rites and rituals for which it is acceptable to spend a lot of money to elevate an event; a funeral is not one of them.[9] It does not matter how much money we have, or where we live. The deceased is dressed in simple garments and placed in a simple, plain pine casket. There is no embalming, which costs extra money and unnaturally delays decomposition.[10] We are born from "dust" and return to "dust"; this is true for all of us, no matter who we are.[11]

My father's all-time favorite sermon was given by one of my childhood rabbis, Avis Miller. She spoke about "showing up for each other" as one of Judaism's core principles. Given that a Jewish funeral is a simple affair, there is only one task for the attendee, and that is to show up—either for the deceased as a final act of gratitude for all that they meant to you, and for the mourners, who will need you to carry them forward. In fact, funerals are supposed to be short so that the greatest number of people can attend, even those who need to go to work or back home to care for children.

Showing up for a funeral is considered an imperative, as it is an indicator of respect both for the deceased and for their family members. This is manifested most clearly after the service and burial have ended. As the mourners leave the grave, community members form two parallel lines that the mourners walk through. This is a physical representation of the commitment to surround mourners with love in the days, weeks, and months to come.

After the funeral

Even when the burial is over, our brains make it difficult to quickly return to our daily lives. Judaism recognizes that for mourners there's a new normal, and in order to live in it, mourners need time to process their loss. With that in mind, the ancient rabbis created the practice of *shiva*, a Hebrew word meaning "seven." Shiva is the week-long period after the funeral, during which mourners remain at home as much as possible, in order to be able to experience the full range of grief-fueled emotions: sadness, anger, fear, confusion, gratitude.

At shiva for my father, we participated in many traditional behaviors intended to remind us and those around us that we were in mourning. We did not wear leather shoes, historically a symbol of luxury. We sat on low benches, or on couches from which cushions have been removed, a reminder of our low energy. We didn't cut our hair, shave, or use cosmetics. We covered the mirrors in the home to discourage vanity and encourage inner reflection. While these specific traditions may not be meaningful to you, it is helpful for the community to witness your displaying outwardly what you are feeling inwardly. Most community members will be going about their regular lives when they are not with you; seeing you low on the floor, or with a few days' growth of beard, will remind them that you are not okay.

The truth is that I didn't need reminding that my father was gone. The pain was ever-present. But I did appreciate the outward manifestations of what I was feeling inside. And visitors, coming into the shiva house from a regular day at work or school, often needed the visual reminder as well.

When someone close to us has died, our inclination may be to deflect the sadness that can sometimes overwhelm us. But sorrow does not just dissipate; it lodges and festers in our bodies. We need a way to encounter our mourning, to move through it, and to allow our community to help us mourn. Whether you use traditional shiva rituals in your time of mourning or create others, such as placing photographs of the deceased throughout the house, what is important is to have rituals and to let your loved ones know what they are. In this way, they will recognize when you are making use of them and will offer the care you need.

Some people may get antsy during such a long stretch of mourning, especially if the person who died had been ill and dying over a long period of time. While this is understandable, shiva forces people to start to process their loss rather than to sublimate it. Shiva can also be a time of connection among family members, some of whom may otherwise rarely see each other. For those who do not get bereavement leave, having the boundary of shiva may inspire your boss to give you a little bit more time before forcing you to return to work.

The entire shiva process is facilitated by friends and family who visit the home regularly, bringing food and words of comfort, setting up and cleaning up as necessary, dealing with annoying visitors, and simply being present. Visitors at the house of mourning have specific responsibilities, including sharing condolences and memories of the deceased. They absolutely should not expect to be hosted! The mourners' job is to mourn, and visitors help to facilitate that process.

Mourners end shiva with a walk around the block, a physical representation of the beginning of a return to work, school, and the new normal that is their life without their loved one. This secondary period of mourning, called *shloshim* (the Hebrew word for "thirty") lasts another twenty-three days after shiva, for a total of thirty days. Mourners return to work and no longer sit on low stools. They may come and go from home as they wish. A few restrictions remain; after my father died, for instance, I did not attend parties for some time. I did this to remind myself of my loss and also because I didn't want my grief to take away from the joy of the people celebrating.

After shloshim, mourning continues for another eleven or twelve months, but at a lower level of intensity. To be clear, according to traditional strictures, mourning would only continue this long for a parent. If one has lost a child, sibling, or spouse, then after shloshim, mourning is over. This might seem surprising: Should we not mourn a child more than a parent, who (we hope) has lived a long life? Remember that two thousand years ago, when many of these laws originated, infant and child mortality were much more common. Parents did not have the capacity to mourn for an entire year, and neither did older siblings. Today in the United States, even by age eighty, only 18 percent of parents have experienced the death of a child. Only 7 percent of children or young adults have lost a sibling.[12] Since the death of a child is so rare in contemporary times—and of course so deeply painful—many of the people with whom I work choose to use Jewish ritual to mourn a "first-degree" relative for the full year.

How do we mourn during this time in which we have come more fully into the "new normal?" Jewish tradition offers a few options.

- Spend time regularly with a group of people who knew your loved one personally and with whom you can mourn.

- Spend time regularly with a group of people who are also in mourning, because you will most likely have some insight into what each of you is going through.

- Choose a specific poem or prayer to read every day, to be reminded of your loved one.

- Read a book on a topic important to or cherished by your loved one.

- Perform ongoing and specific good deeds or other practices that your loved one would have appreciated, and in their memory.

- Give regularly to a charity that had meaning for your loved one.

Whatever you choose to do, our tradition would have you do it regularly. On some days you will feel your loved one's presence; on others, you may be annoyed at having to take time away from daily life, and may even think to yourself, "My loved one would not have wanted me to be performing this ritual. They would want me to get back to normal." Remember that these traditions are only partially for your loved one. More than anything else, they are for *you*—to help you process your grief, learn whatever you can from the person who died, teach your friends and family about that person, and remind your community that the "normal" of the past no longer exists for you.

How do I mourn a terrible person?

Awful people—those who are physically and verbally abusive, selfish, bigoted—have existed since humans were created. Those of us who are mourning a terrible person are not alone, even in our suffering. Other people are connected to terrible people who die, and we, the living, have to figure out how to remember them. Judaism recommends that we enact the same rituals of mourning even for the most awful person. Sometimes after a person is dead, a mourner is finally able to find the sparks of something redeeming in the deceased's life, which may provide some solace. Sara Sherbill wrote the following in an article about her abusive father.

> To tell you the truth, I'm not mad my father's gone. In his
> later years, his experience of life was mostly relegated
> to suffering—and to making those around him suffer, too.
> Death is always supposed to be a tragedy, the worst
> thing that could happen. But I do not feel that way. It is
> only now that my father is occupying another realm, one
> far away from Earth, that I can feel his love.[13]

Sometimes, mourners are not even able to acknowledge publicly what they survived until after an abusive or difficult family member has died. Public mourning rituals that acknowledge these unpleasant truths, such as talking about it (when appropriate) or writing honestly about the relationship, may be freeing.

The most important thing is for mourners to take care of themselves psychologically, and not perform any rituals that might further traumatize them. While for some that may mean sitting at home and thinking about an abusive parent who has died, for others it may mean joining a support group for people who have had abusive parents. Either might be meaningful, but the latter could be more useful in helping mourners know they are not alone.

Mourning for a whole people

A story, perhaps apocryphal, is told of Napoleon, who once walked the streets of Jerusalem in the dead of summer. He noticed Jews sitting in sackcloth and ashes on the ground, weeping. And he asked his commanders, "Why do these Jews weep?"

"They are mourning their Temple," his associates replied, "and their people sent into exile."

"That is terrible!" Napoleon said. "Did we destroy it? When did it fall?"

"Oh, no," the soldiers said. "Their Temple was destroyed eighteen hundred years ago. But once a year, these Jews still mourn."

Napoleon paused, and then responded: "A people that almost two millennia later continues to mourn a Temple destroyed and a people dispersed is a people that will survive for two millennia into the future."

Jews mourn not only those we have personally loved and lost, or those we knew. We also mourn people we never met, whose names we will never know, who died over the course of Jewish history.

We have major communal days of mourning three times a year. On one of these days, we mourn those who were killed in the Shoah (the Hebrew word for the Holocaust), in which six million Jews were murdered by the Nazis and their accomplices. On another, we mourn those who were killed defending the State of Israel, or who were murdered in terrorist bombings. The third of these days of mourning is the one that Napoleon encountered, called Tisha B'Av (the ninth day of the month of Av). It is a fast day on which we remember all the other terrible things that have happened to the Jewish people—torture, exile, destruction, murder—over our history. For twenty-five hours, we are asked to remember it all.

Remembering alone, by yourself, is not enough; There are specific communal rituals as well. On Tisha B'Av there is no eating, drinking, or sex. There is no bathing or swimming. We sit on the ground and read passages that bring us back to that moment of complete brokenness, in Jerusalem, in 70 CE.

> Alas! Lonely sits the city once great with people!...
> Bitterly she weeps in the night, her cheeks wet with tears....
> Judah has gone into exile....
> When she settled among the nations, she found no rest.
> All her pursuers overtook her in narrow places.
> Zion's roads are in mourning, empty of festival pilgrims.
> All her gates are deserted....[14]

What are the identities that you claim most proudly? A religion? Nationality? LGBTQIA+? Union member? What if there were one day a year in which you and others in your community came together to mourn all of those dear to you who have died, all you have lost? On the other 364 days, *celebrate* your identity. On the other 364 days, remember people from *other* identities who struggle in the fight for their rights. One day a year is about loss in your group alone. Imagine if Memorial Day were observed by *all* Americans, those with a family member or friend who died for the sake of our country, those without that grave of a loss, but all of us who reap the benefits of freedom because of the ultimate sacrifice made by others.

Group mourning rituals remind us not only that we are not alone, but also that we stand on the shoulders of others who have died so that we can live today. Our communal Jewish mourning rituals are both vertical and horizontal in time. They stretch backward through history and will also be marked in the future, as well. They also are marked on the same day by Jews worldwide. Communal mourning can serve to build gratitude for all that has happened in the past and strengthen resolve for all that you may accomplish in the future. This is what Tisha B'Av is to the Jewish people. It is what the Trans Day of Remembrance has become for the trans community. This is what a ritual of mourning could be for your identities and communities..

Paradoxically, Tisha B'Av, the Jewish day of communal mourning, is in some ways also a day of celebration. It is a day on which we mourn all our losses but also mark our resilience. There is a story told of four rabbis walking through ancient Jerusalem after the destruction of the Temple, the holiest site for the Jewish people. The embers of the Temple were still burning, and the bodies of the dead had not yet all been counted. The rabbis could hear their Roman enemies advancing upon them. Three of the rabbis started weeping. The fourth rabbi laughed. "How can you laugh in this terrible moment?" the three rabbis asked, tearing their clothing in a sign of mourning. "The Romans have conquered us!"

The laughing one, Rabbi Akiva, responded in the same way that tens of thousands of Jews have over the course of our history: We have been broken before, and we have risen from the ashes. This time, too, we will rise.[15] Ultimately, Rabbi Akiva himself was murdered by the Romans, flayed alive for the crime of teaching Jewish texts. But he understood that resilience can be both an individual and a communal experience. This resonates with the research of the psychologists Marshall Duke, Amber Lazarus, and Robyn Fivush, who have shown that children who know their family stories—and especially what they call the "oscillating narrative" of good times and difficult ones—are more resilient than those who do not.[16]

Our tradition teaches that the messiah, the harbinger of a healed, perfect future, will be born on Tisha B'av. Maybe you believe in a messiah, maybe you don't. It is astonishing that it is this day of fasting and of sackcloth and ashes on which our imagined redeemer will be born, and not another holiday such as our Passover holiday of liberation. It reminds us of how critical the process of mourning is for us as individuals, as a community, and as a people.

Tisha B'Av is twenty-five hours long, beginning at sundown and ending an hour after sundown a day later. It begins in deep mourning, with people sitting on the floor by candlelight, weeping in sadness. No one is even supposed to greet each other. By midafternoon the next day, the mood starts to shift. People rise from the ground and are allowed to converse with each other. A sense of hope returns, as reflected in the words we say to each other and the words we chant from our sacred texts. *Nachum*, we say: comfort. We find comfort. We find hope.

The Jewish mourning cycle is designed not only to hold us in our desolation but to slowly ease us back into the world, with its full cacophony of emotions, including joy, gratitude, and hope. "They who sow in tears," one sacred text teaches, "shall reap with songs of joy."[17] It is only when we go through the process of true mourning that we can come out on the other side, ready to reengage with the world in a new way, in the "new normal."

A story is told of a rabbi named Joshua who had a number of students who were in prolonged grief after the destruction of the

Temple. Joshua asked them, "Why aren't you drinking wine or eating meat?"

They said, "How can we, when we used both in the Temple in times of joy? The Temple is now destroyed!"

"That's true," Joshua said, "and perhaps we also shouldn't eat bread, since there were offerings of bread in the Temple that we can no longer make."

They said, "You are correct."

"And no produce either," he said, "because we used to celebrate our harvest by bringing fruit to the Temple, as well."

"Yes!" they agreed.

"And no water, either," said Joshua, "because we used water on one of the most joyous days of the year in the Temple."

The students were silent, since they realized they couldn't live without water.

"My children," Joshua taught, "not to mourn at all is impossible. But to mourn excessively is also impossible."

So Joshua's students compromised. They could eat bread, produce, and meat; they could drink both water and wine. They could even celebrate all their holidays and be joyous in their lives. But a tiny part of their homes, 1.5 square feet, would forever remain unfinished, a marker of their sadness. It would be a scar, a reminder that they had lived through the trauma, emerged on the other side and had not forgotten.[18]

You and I can emerge out of mourning into a new normal. My father passed away almost twenty years ago, but I still think about him all the time. Jewish practice acknowledges that just because someone has been dead for a long time does not mean that they have been forgotten. There are five specific times during the year during which we honor and remember people close to us who have died. Four of the times are on holidays, times when we might be celebrating with our loved one, were they still alive, and once is on the anniversary of the day of their death. In my family, on these days, we talk about the person who has died, and we light a special *yahrzeit* candle that burns for at least twenty-four hours. We do special readings in memory of the person who has died and give money to charity in their memory. Sometimes, we go to communal memorial services to remember those who have died, so that we do not have to mourn alone. You might want to find people to mourn with on specific dates after the death of a loved one. It might be their death date, as is the Jewish tradition, or perhaps their birthday, or the opening day of a sports season that they loved. The sadness around a death is not meant to be private. There are others who have also lost people; we can mourn together.

Gratitude in the face of death

Jewish practice forces us to recognize that everyone we love is going to die, and that we are, as well. The goal and the hope is that it makes us grateful for every moment—or at least as many of them as we can manage.

On the Jewish holiday of Yom Kippur, we do the work of looking inside and right-sizing ourselves; of understanding how finite it all is, of letting go of the hurt and the anger that only serves to hold us back. We say aloud: "Our time together is finite, and I'm working as hard as I can to make it count." Sometimes, I cannot get there. I get stuck in the world of what-if statements, always anticipating the next bad thing. Instead of feeling joy at getting to take my son for a milkshake, walking home in the cool end-of-summer evening, there's an alarm going off in my head—this is almost over . . . this is almost over . . . this is almost over. The alarm keeps me from enjoying this sacred moment. This happens to me on vacation. When the plane takes off, on the way *there*, I'm already thinking, "This is already over." It's an unhealthy, unhelpful, joy-blocking way to be. Instead, why not appreciate every moment, as fleeting as it is?

A few years ago, my youngest daughter, Natalia, celebrated her bat mitzvah (a Jewish coming-of-age ceremony, marked at age twelve or thirteen) with a party at the same Candy Cane City where we celebrated my father's brief remission sixteen years earlier. We had a "puppy party" with puppies from a local animal shelter, excellent pizza, a little bit of henna for temporary tattoos, and a hora. My dad would have loved it.

During the party, I was overwhelmed by disparate feelings. There was the deep joy of Natalia's bat mitzvah itself. I also had my "1.5-square-feet" moment, looking at the backstop, angry that my dad didn't live to meet Natalia, or to see my other two children grow up. Anger, a secondary emotion, was covering up the sadness that I was feeling inside.

I took a breath and looked at the community around me. They had carried me from my father's death to this moment and they would carry me going forward. And I them. We would show up not just for the pizza but also for the "club of sh*t," which is what one of my mom's closest friends called my father's funeral. We'd show up for the full cacophony of it all. To live is to die. But is also to be *alive*.

I turned from the backstop to face the field, filled with my loved ones. And I walked forward.

The Way Forward

Before we say goodbye, let's reflect for a minute on what we've explored together—the deep and enduring wisdom of Jewish tradition, and how it can guide us toward a life of purpose and connection. Each of the "Ways"—from Chesed to Shabbat, from Am to Tzedek—has deepened my understanding of what it means to live a meaningful life within the framework of Judaism. These paths are not isolated; they weave together a tapestry of purpose, allowing us to engage with our traditions, our communities, and the world around us and elevate the mundane into something sacred. *The Jewish Way to a Good Life* is an invitation to engage with ancient principles and teachings that resonate with our modern lives. It's about building a life rooted in kindness, community, and justice, while also embracing the joy, rest, and learning that sustain us.

This journey isn't limited to Jews. As I've learned throughout my career, there is so much in Judaism that resonates beyond our community. I've seen people from all walks of life have their first shabbat dinner, relax into it, and connect with something simultaneously ancient and personally meaningful. This book is an invitation for you, regardless of your background, to hold on to the teachings that speak to you most.

Judaism has survived for millennia because while it is rooted in tradition, it also adapts, challenges, and sustains. We don't always get it right, and our tradition is certainly not without its flaws. But at its core, Judaism offers practices and principles that can guide us through the complexities of modern life, whether we are navigating joy, sorrow, or everyday moments.

As I've walked these paths myself, it has become clear to me that the Jewish way of living is about intention and relationship. It's about how we treat others, how we honor ourselves, and how we seek to improve the world. When I teach about chesed or ahava, I'm not just speaking in abstract terms. I'm inviting you to embrace these values and put them into action, and in doing so, to see how acts of lovingkindness and love itself can be transformative.

This journey is ongoing. As I've found meaning in Judaism over my lifetime, I've learned that these teachings are not static. They grow with us as we change, adapt, and evolve. At points throughout our life, we pick some up and drop others. The same holds true for you.

Whether you are Jewish, curious about Judaism, or simply looking for inspiration to enrich your life, I hope this book has given you a taste of what's possible. Incorporate what works for you. And remember, it's the little things—the daily moments of joy and caring for our bodies—that create a life of meaning.

Ultimately, Judaism has taught me that a meaningful life doesn't just happen. It's something we build, piece by piece, day by day. As you walk your own path, may you find the practices that sustain you, inspire you, and connect you to a world greater than yourself. And when you're ready, may you pass them on.

Notes

The Way of . . .

1. Proverbs 3:18.
2. "Jewish Population Rises to 15.7 Million Worldwide in 2023," The Jewish Agency for Israel, September 15, 2023, jewishagency.org/jewish-population-rises-to-15-7-million-worldwide-in-2023.
3. Berachot 16b.
4. "Birkat Hachodesh," Sefaria.org, accessed October 2, 2024.
5. Aaron Earls, "Americans' Views of Life's Meaning and Purpose Are Changing," Lifeway Research, April 6, 2021, research.lifeway.com/2021/04/06/americans-views-of-lifes-meaning-and-purpose-are-changing.
6. "Jewish Americans in 2020," Pew Research Center, May 11, 2021, pewresearch.org/religion/2021/05/11/jewish-americans-in-2020.
7. Psalms 19:15.

1   The Way of *Chesed*: Acts of Lovingkindness

1. Pirkei Avot 1:2.
2. "What is Chesed?," PJ Library, June 16, 2020, pjlibrary.org/beyond-books/pjblog/june-2020/what-is-chesed.
3. Sota 14a, Mishnah Peah 1:1.
4. Anne Lamott, *Bird by Bird: Some Instructions on Writing and Life* (Anchor Books, 2019).
5. Pirkei Avot 2:21.
6. Psalms 89:3.
7. Netivot Olam, Path of Loving Your Neighbor, 1:2, 4.
8. Cynthia Griffith, "The Numbers Don't Lie: Drug Addiction is Not a Leading Cause of Homelessness," Invisible People, January 14, 2022, invisiblepeople.tv/the-numbers-dont-lie-drug-addiction-is-not-a-leading-cause-of-homelessness.
9. Jerusalem Talmud Gittin 5:9.
10. Pirkei Avot 4:2.

11. Steve Siegle, "The art of kindness," Mayo Clinic Health System, August 17, 2023, mayoclinichealthsystem.org/hometown-health/speaking-of-health/the-art-of-kindness.

12. Genesis Rabbah 12:15. This text is actually about balancing rachamim/compassion and dim/strict judgment. I have included it here because the Venn diagram of compassion and chesed overlap substantially, and the idea of balancing lovingkindness and strict judgment is a core Kabbalistic idea.

13. Rabbi Shaya Karlinsky, "Chapter 1: Mishna 2: Part 4," Torah.org, accessed October 7, 2024, torah.org/learning/maharal-p1m2part4.

14. Deuteronomy 16:16–17, Chagiga 1:1.

15. Pirkei Avot 5:7.

2 The Way of *Ahava*: Love + Sex

1. Leviticus 19:18.

2. Bava Metzia 62a.

3. Dr. Andleeb Asghar, "The science of self-love: the evidence-based benefits of loving yourself," Ness Labs, accessed October 7, 2024, nesslabs.com/self-love.

4. Jannik Lindner, "Study Reveals Impactful Self Love Statistics on Mental Health," Gitnux.org, July 17, 2024, gitnux.org/self-love-statistics.

5. Nguyen Tan Dat et al., "Relationship between self-esteem and suicidal ideation before and during COVID-19 in a non-clinical sample," *Frontiers in Psychiatry* 14 (2023).

6. Numbers 13:27.

7. Numbers 13:33.

8. "Sh'lach, Siman 7," Sefaria.org, accessed October 7, 2024.

9. "Self-Improvement Market in U.S. Worth $9.6 Billion," Archive.today, September 21, 2006, archive.ph/20070421220629/http:/www.prwebdirect.com/releases/2006/9/prweb440011.php#selection-299.0-306.0.

10. II Samuel 1:26.

11. Pirkei Avot 1:6.

12. Proverbs 27:17.

13. Bereshit Rabbah 54:3.

14. Avot d'Rabbi Natan 8:3.

15. Proverbs 18:24.

16. Song of Songs 8:6.

17. Mishnah Ketubot 5:6.

18. Maria Peña, "The Ketubah, An Ornate Jewish Marriage Tradition," Library of Congress Blogs, June 9, 2023, blogs.loc.gov/loc/2023/06/the-ketubah-an-ornate-jewish-marriage-tradition.

19. Rashi on Genesis 2:18.

20. Sanhedrin 76b.

21. Kedushat Levi, Genesis, Chayei Sara 24:67.

22. Song of Songs 1:2.

23. Song of Songs 2:3–5.

24. Nachmanides, Iggeret HaKodesh.

25. Eruvin 100b.

26. Brachot 62a.

27. Ketubot 62a.

28. Ketubot 61a.

29. Zohar text.

30. Yoma 18b.

31. Rabbi Gershon Winkler, "What Does Judaism Say About Love?," *Moment*, September/October 2010, 24.

32. Rabbi David G. Winship, "Falling in Love," Sefaria.org, accessed October 9, 2024.

33. Ibn Ezra on Leviticus 19:17.

34. Rabbi Yosef Bechor Shor on Leviticus 19:17.

35. Rashbam on Leviticus 19:17.

36. Kli Yakar on Leviticus 19:17

37. Gavriel Goldfeder, "Why the Torah doesn't tell you to love your parents?," Sefaria.org, accessed October 9, 2024.

38. Song of Songs 8:6.

39. "Steinsaltz on Song of Songs 8:6," Sefaria.org, accessed October 9, 2024.

40. Shabbat 31a.

3　The Way of *Simcha*: Happiness + Celebration

1. Kenneth M. Cramer and Hailey Pawsey, "Happiness and sense of community belonging in the world value survey," *Current Research in Ecological and Social Psychology* 4 (2023).

2.   Kohelet 2:1–2 and 8:15; Isaiah 22:13; Shabbat 30b on Simcha shel Mitzvah.

3.   "Giving thanks can make you happier," Harvard Health Publishing, August 14, 2021, health.harvard.edu/healthbeat/giving-thanks-can-make-you-happier.

4.   Ciro Conversano et al., "Optimism and Its Impact on Mental and Physical Well-Being," *Clinical Practice & Epidemiology in Mental Health* 6 (2010): 25–29.

5.   Mary Oliver, "Poem 133: The Summer Day," Library of Congress, accessed October 9, 2024, loc.gov/programs/poetry-and-literature/poet-laureate/poet-laureate-projects/poetry-180/all-poems/item/poetry-180-133/the-summer-day.

6.   Taanit 22a.

7.   Deuteronomy 16:13–15.

8.   Rambam, Mishneh Torah, Rest on a Holiday 6:18.

9.   Elizabeth W. Dunn et al., "Prosocial Spending and Happiness: Using Money to Benefit Others Pays Off," *Current Directions in Psychological Science* 23, no.1 (2014): 41–47.

10.   Exodus 4:14.

11.   Yalkut Shimoni on Torah 172.

12.   Yehuda Amichai, "A Man in His Life."

13.   Ketubot 17a.

14.   Psalms 2:11, Brachot 30b.

15.   Avot D'rabbi Natan 34:10; Malbim commentary on sasson/simcha; Rabbi Paul Kipnes and Michelle November, MSSW, *Jewish Spiritual Parenting: Wisdom, Activities, Rituals and Prayers for Raising Children with Spiritual Balance and Emotional Wholeness* (Jewish Lights Publishing, 2015), 167–69.

16.   Soyoung Q. Park et al., "A neural link between generosity and happiness," *Nature Communications* 8, no. 15964 (2017).

17.   Numbers 11:4–6.

18.   Likutei Moharan, Part II, Torah 23:1.

19.   Katy Duke, "Faking happiness at work can make you ill," *BMJ* 332, no. 747 (2006):.

20.   Gwyneth Rees, "After decades of debate, why forcing yourself to smile will actually make you feel happier," The i Paper, December 2, 2022, inews.co.uk/inews-lifestyle/decades-debate-forcing-smile-happier-2003645.

21. Paula M. Loveday, Geoff P. Lovell, Christian M. Jones, "The Best Possible Selves Intervention: A Review of the Literature to Evaluate Efficacy and Guide Future Research," *Journal of Happiness Studies* 19 (2018): 607–28.

22. Susan Shain, "How to Be More Optimistic," *The New York Times*, February 18, 2020, nytimes.com/2020/02/18/smarter-living/how-to-be-more-optimistic.html.

4 The Way of *Guf*: The Body

1. Ta'anit 20a-b.

2. Midrash Tehillim 18:2.

3. Mishneh Torah Human Dispositions 4:1.

4. Orach hayim 80.1.

5. Otzar Midrashim, Midrash Temurah 1.

6. Rambam Hilchot Deot 4:1.

7. Kitzur Shulchan Aruch 32:14.

8. Shulchan Aruch, Yoreh De'ah 336.

9. Yoma 83a, Proverbs 14:10.

10. Avodah zarah 30b.

11. Elliot N. Dorff, *Matters of Life and Death: A Jewish Approach to Modern Medical Ethics* (Jewish Publication Society, 2003), 253.

12. Morot L'Halakha, "Human Papilloma Virus (HPV) Vaccination – Halakhic Transgression or Obligation? Sharon Galper–Grossman," Sefaria.org, accessed October 9, 2024.

13. Kevin D. Hall et al., "Ultra-Processed Diets Cause Excess Calorie Intake and Weight Gain: An Inpatient Randomized Controlled Trial of *Ad Libitum* Food Intake," *Cell Metabolism* 30, no. 1 (2019): 67–77.

14. Alice Callahan, "Is It Bad to Eat Late at Night?," *The New York Times*, December 19, 2023.

15. Pirke Avot 3:3.

16. Kiddushin 40b.

17. Jerusalem Talmud, Kiddushin 4:12.

18. Bert Musschenga, "Is There a Problem With False Hope?," *Journal of Medicine and Philosophy* 44, no. 4 (2019): 423–41.

19. Berakhot 5b.

20. David Fouchet et al., "Visiting Sick People: Is It Really Detrimental to Our Health?," *PLOS One* 3, no. 6 (2008).

21. Angela Epstein, "The proof that visiting people in hospital really does them good," *Daily Mail*, October 16, 2006, dailymail.co.uk/health/article-410783/ The-proof-visiting-people-hospital-really-does-good.html.

22. "Half of World's Population Will Experience a Mental Health Disorder," Harvard Medical School, July 31, 2023, hms.harvard.edu/news/ half-worlds-population-will-experience-mental-health-disorder.

23. Lizzie Duszynski-Goodman, "Mental Health Statistics and Facts," *Forbes*, February 21, 2024, forbes.com/health/mind/mental-health-statistics.

24. Yoma 75a.

25. Elizabeth Midlarsky et al., "Religion, Ethnicity, and Attitudes Toward Psychotherapy," *Journal of Religion and Health* 51 (2012): 498–506.

26. Jay Michaelson, *The Gate of Tears: Sadness and the Spiritual Path* (Ben Yehuda Press, 2015).

27. I Samuel 16.

28. Sandro Galea, "Chronic Pain and the Health of Populations," Boston University School of Public Health, September 24, 2017, bu.edu/sph/news/articles/2017/ chronic-pain-and-the-health-of-populations.

29. Mishnah Brachot 9:3.

30. Proverbs 13:12.

31. Pesachim 64b.

32. Joshua 2:1.

33. Pesachim 64 a–b.

5 The Way of *Mamon*: Money

1. Khanyi Mlaba, "The Richest 1% Own Almost Half the World's Wealth & 9 Other Mind-Blowing Facts on Wealth Inequality," Global Citizen, January 19, 2023, globalcitizen.org/en/content/wealth-inequality-oxfam-billionaires-elon-musk.

2. I took these quotes, and indeed the entire concept of "Money Messages," from 21/64, an organization providing multigenerational advising, facilitation, and training for next-generation engagement.

3. Anand Giridharadas, "The Thriving World, the Wilting World, and You," Medium, July 31, 2015, medium.com/@AnandWrites/ the-thriving-world-the-wilting-world-and-you-209ffc24ab90.

4. Deuteronomy 8:12–18.

5. Rabbi John L. Rosove, "7 Questions You'll Be Asked By the Heavenly Tribunal," Reformjudaism.org, reformjudaism.org/7-questions-youll-be-asked-heavenly-tribunal, accessed October 9, 2024.

6. Ecclesiastes 4:4.

7.   Isaiah 58:3.

8. Sanhedrin 21b.

9. Bereshit Rabbah 9:7.

10. Genesis Rabbah 16:8.

11. Avot D'rabbi Natan 11:1.

12. Genesis 2:5.

13. Isaiah 2:4.

14. Nedarim 49b.

15. Pirkei Avot 2:2, Nedarim 49b, Rabbeinu Yonah, on Pirkei Avot 1:10:1.

16. Brachot 32a.

17. Ketubot 5:5.

18. Berachot 35b, Avot 2:5, Avot 4:10.

19. Hibah Shariff, "Schwab's Modern Wealth Survey Reveals Nearly Half of Americans Feel Wealthy . . . But With a Twist: They Don't Measure It in Dollars & Cents," Charles Schwab Corporation, June 13, 2023, pressroom.aboutschwab.com/press-releases/press-release/2023/Schwabs-Modern-Wealth-Survey-Reveals-Nearly-Half-of-Americans-Feel-WealthyBut-With-a-Twist-They-Dont-Measure-It-in-Dollars--Cents/default.aspx.

20. Daniel Glaser, "Rich is relative: how well-off do you feel?," *The Guardian*, May 14, 2017; "Taking A Closer Look at Social Comparison Theory," American Psychological Association, April 19, 2018, apa.org/pubs/highlights/spotlight/issue-115.

21. Caroline Beaton, "Why You Feel Richer or Poorer Than You Really Are," *The Cut*, August 3, 2017.

22. Shabbat 25b.

23. Kohelet Rabbah, 1:13.

24. Annie Leonard, "Story of Stuff, Referenced and Annotated Script," storyofstuff.org/wp-content/uploads/2020/01/StoryofStuff_AnnotatedScript.pdf.

25. Ivana Saric, "U.S. hits new low in World Happiness Report," Axios, March 19, 2024, axios.com/2024/03/20/world-happiness-america-low-list-countries.

26. Kohelet 5:10–14.

27. Leviticus Rabbah 34:7.

28. Michael Blanding, "Why Giving to Others Makes Us Happy," Working Knowledge, Harvard Business School, August 15, 2023, hbswk.hbs.edu/item/why-giving-to-others-makes-us-happy.

29. Elizabeth Dunn and Chris Courtney, "Does More Money Really Make Us More Happy?," *Harvard Business Review*, September 14, 2020, hbr.org/2020/09/does-more-money-really-makes-us-more-happy.

30. "What Really Lowers Crime," NV.gov Department of Sentencing Policy, August 24, 2022, sentencing.nv.gov/uploadedFiles/sentencingnvgov/content/Meetings/2022/08.24.22%20NSC%20Mtg.%20Agenda%20Item%208%20PFJ%20What%20Really%20Lowers%20Crime.pdf.

31. Leah Goggins, "Here's Where Your Girl Scout Cookie Money Actually Goes," EatingWell, February 28, 2022, eatingwell.com/article/7949852/where-does-girl-scout-cookie-money-go.

32. Nathan Dietz, "Social Connectedness and Generosity: A Look at How Associational Life and Social Connections Influence Volunteering and Giving (and Vice Versa)," University of Maryland School of Public Policy, Do Good Institute, January 11, 2024, dogood.umd.edu/research-impact/publications/social-connectedness-and-generosity-look-how-associational-life-and.

33. Jerusalem Talmud, Kiddushin, 4:12

34. Mishnah Berakhot 9:5; "Collaborative Consumption: It is Jew-ish," Sefaria.org, accessed October 10, 2024.

35. Shulchan Aruch Choshen Mishpat 228:4.

36. Deuteronomy 17:16–18.

37. Nedarim 38a.

6 The Way of *Limud*: Education

1. "Jewish Americans in 2020," Pew Research Center, May 11, 2021, pewresearch.org/religion/2021/05/11/jewish-community-and-connectedness.

2. Vanessa L. Ochs, "What Makes a Jewish Home Jewish?," *CrossCurrents* 49, no. 4 (Winter 1999/2000): 491–510.

3. Elka Torpey, "Measuring the value of education," U.S. Bureau of Labor Statistics, April 2018, bls.gov/careeroutlook/2018/data-on-display/education-pays.htm.

4. Orit Kent and Allison Cook, "Three Partners in Study: Two People and a Text," *Sh'ma* (2012).

5. Bava Metzia 84a.

6. Bradley Shavit Artson, "How Do We Speak to Each Other? Like one person with one heart," *Times of Israel*, September 30, 2015, blogs.timesofisrael.com/ like-one-person-with-one-heart-how-do-we-speak-to-each-other.

7. Shandra Furtado, "The Important Relationship between Forests and Fire," *American Forests*, April 5, 2016, americanforests.org/article/ the-important-relationship-between-forests-and-fire.

8. Angela Haupt, "How to Actually Change Someone's Mind," *TIME*, October 26, 2022.

9. Elizabeth Kolbert, "Why Facts Don't Change Our Minds," *The New Yorker*, February 19, 2017.

10. Bava Metzia 59b.

11. Berachot 61b.

12. Kiddushin 29a. The text that I interpret as "commit to raising them as Jews" is actually about circumcision.

13. Kiddushin 30b.

14. Mishneh Torah, Torah Study 2:1.

15. "Early Warning! Why Reading by the End of Third Grade Matters," Annie E. Casey Foundation, January 1, 2010, aecf.org/resources/ early-warning-why-reading-by-the-end-of-third-grade-matters.

16. Shulchan Aruch, Yoreh De'ah, 245:7.

17. Baba Batra 21a.

18. Brachot 27b–28a.

19. Baba Batra 21a.

20. Baba Metzia 59b.

21. Donald Sheff, "Izzy, Did You Ask a Good Question Today?," *The New York Times*, January 19, 1988, nytimes.com/1988/01/19/opinion/l-izzy-did-you-ask-a-good-question-today-712388.html.

22. Pirke Avot 4:1.

23. Niddah 30b.

24. Pirke Avot 1:16, 5:21.

25. Rachel Wu and Carla Strickland-Hughes, "Think you're too old to learn new tricks?," *Scientific American*, July 17, 2019, blogs.scientificamerican.com/ observations/think-youre-too-old-to-learn-new-tricks.

26. "Does Higher Learning Combat Dementia?," Johns Hopkins Medicine, accessed October 10, 2024, hopkinsmedicine.org/health/wellness-and-prevention/does-higher-learning-combat-dementia.

27. Berachot 58b.

28. Proverbs 22:6.

29. Kiddushin 29b.

30. Kiddushin 40b.

31. Pirke Avot 6:1.

32. Midrash Tanhuma Mishpatim 2.

33. All quotes from bettertogether.org.

34. Vayikra Rabbah 4:6.

35. Rebecca Solnit, "The Ideology of Isolation," *Harper's*, July 2016, harpers.org/archive/2016/07/the-ideology-of-isolation/?single=1.

36. Pirke Avot 1:15.

37. John T. Cacioppo and William Patrick, *Loneliness: Human Nature and the Need for Social Connection* (W. W. Norton & Company, 2009).

38. Agnes Callard, "The Problem of Marital Loneliness," *The New Yorker*, September 25, 2021.

39. Louise C. Hawkley et al., "Loneliness from young adulthood to old age: Explaining age differences in loneliness," *International Journal of Behavioral Development* 46, no. 1 (2022): 39–49.

40. Chagiga 14a.

41. Sanhedrin 17b.

42. Yekum Purkan, Shabbat Musaf.

43. Sforno on Numbers 24:5.

44. Shulchan Aruch Orech Chaim 90:4.

45. Berachot 27b–28a.

46. Deuteronomy 29:9–11.

8 The Way of *Tzedek*: Justice

1. Mishnah Pesachim 10:5, cited in the Passover Haggadah.

2. Genesis 38:26.

3. Bava Batra 88b.

4. Leviticus 19:15.

5. Sanhedrin 32b.

6. Proverbs 10:25.

7.   "Glossary of Terms," Learn Kabbalah, accessed October 10, 2024, learnkabbalah.com/glossary-of-terms.

8.   Mishnah Sanhedrin 8:6–7.

9.   Isaiah 57:14–58:14.

10.   Jeremiah 22:3.

11.   Jeremiah 38:6, 1 Kings 22:26-27, Amos 7:12–13, Ezekiel 12:1–3, among others.

12.   Abraham Joshua Heschel, *Abraham Joshua Heschel: Essential Writings*, ed. Susannah Heschel (Orbis Books, 2011).

13.   Yoma 9b.

14.   Derech Eretz, Perek Shalom.

15.   Sanhedrin 96b.

16.   Pirke Avot 4:19.

17.   Shabbat 54b.

18.   Emma Lazarus, "An Epistle to the Hebrews," *The American Hebrew*, November 10, 1882–February 24, 1883.

19.   Gabriela Nietlisbach et al., "Are empathic abilities impaired in posttraumatic stress disorder?," *Psychological Reports* 106, no. 3 (2010): 832–44.

20.   Midrash Tanhuma Mishpatim 2.

21.   Rav Moshe Feinstein Letter, October 3, 1984.

22.   Rashi on Deuteronomy 16:20.

23.   Ibn Ezra on Deuteronomy 16:20.

24.   Leviticus 19:15.

25.   Mishneh Torah, Sanhedrin 23:9.

26.   One example, from Nedarim 28a, discusses the requirement for Jews to respect local tax laws.

27.   Jeremiah 29:4–7.

28.   I Samuel Chapter 8.

29.   Avoda Zara 4a.

30.   Exodus 23:2.

31.   Tractate Derech Eretz Zuta, Section on Peace 2.

32.   Sanhedrin 6a.

33.   Bereshit Rabbah 8:5.

34.   Deuteronomy 15:4.

35. Exodus 5:1.

36. Exodus 8:15, 8:32, 9:34.

9 The Way of *Shabbat*: Ceasing + Resting

1. Genesis 2:2–3.

2. Abraham Joshua Heschel, *The Sabbath* (New York: Farrar, Straus and Giroux, 1951).

3. Ibid.

4. Shradha Dinesh and Kim Parker, "More than 4 in 10 U.S. workers don't take all their paid time off," Pew Research Center, August 10, 2023, pewresearch.org/short-reads/2023/08/10/more-than-4-in-10-u-s-workers-dont-take-all-their-paid-time-off.

5. Mishnah Shabbat 7:2.

6. Exodus 20:8.

7. Deuteronomy 5:12.

8. Nachmanides on Exodus 20:7.

9. Claudia Skowron, "The 7 Kinds of Rest You Actually Need," *Psychology Today*, December 21, 2022, psychologytoday.com/intl/blog/a-different-kind-of-therapy/202212/the-7-kinds-of-rest-you-need-to-actually-feel-rejuvenated.

10. Deuteronomy 5:14.

11. Deuteronomy 5:14.

12. Allison Zelman, "How Jewish Americans Have Led the Way in Labor Organizing," U.S. Department of Labor Blog, May 24, 2023, blog.dol.gov/2023/05/24/how-jewish-americans-have-led-the-way-in-labor-organizing.

13. "Consumerism and its antisocial effects can be turned on—or off," Association for Psychological Science, April 9, 2012, psychologicalscience.org/news/releases/consumerism-and-its-antisocial-effects-can-be-turned-on-or-off.html.

14. Stephanie Rosenbloom, "But Will It Make You Happy?," *The New York Times*, August 7, 2010, nytimes.com/2010/08/08/business/08consume.html?searchResultPosition=5.

15. Benjamin Alamar and Stanton A. Glantz, "Modeling Addictive Consumption as an Infectious Disease," *Contributions in Economic Analysis & Policy* 5, no. 1 (2006): 1–22.

16. Erica Pandey, "America needs sleep," Axios, May 29, 2022, axios.com/2022/05/24/america-sleep-deprivation-effects-tips.

17. Jocelyn Solis-Moreira, "How Long Does It Really Take to Form a Habit?," *Scientific American*, January 24, 2024, scientificamerican.com/article/ how-long-does-it-really-take-to-form-a-habit.

10 The Way of *Aveilut*: Mourning

1.   Berakhot 16b.

2.   Dimitris Xygalatas, *Ritual: How Seemingly Senseless Acts Make Life Worth Living* (Little, Brown Spark, 2022).

3.   "A surprising employee benefit that often tops the list for women with marginalized identities: Bereavement Leave," Lean In, accessed October 10, 2024, leanin.org/bereavement-at-work.

4.   Emily Batdorf, "Living Paycheck To Paycheck Statistics 2024," *Forbes*, April 2, 2024, forbes.com/advisor/banking/living-paycheck-to-paycheck-statistics-2024.

5.   Bereshit Rabbah 100:7.

6.   Berachot 18a and Shabbat 151b.

7.   Bereshit Rabbah 100:7.

8.   "Death and Debt Survey: Most Americans Would Take on Debt to Plan a Family Member's Funeral," Debt.com, July 23, 2024, debt.com/research/ funeral-debt.

9.   Genesis 3:19.

10. Rambam Hilchot Aveilut.

11. Genesis 3:19.

12. "Grief & Bereavement Key Facts," Evermore, accessed October 10, 2024, evermore.org/key-bereavement-facts.

13. Sara Sherbill, "As a rabbi, he helped others mourn. So why wouldn't his daughter say kaddish for him?," *Forward*, June 13, 2023, forward.com/ culture/550247/mourning-abusive-father-rabbi-fathers-day-cholent.

14. Lamentations 1:1–4.

15. Makkot 24a.

16. Marshall P. Duke et al., "Knowledge of family history as a clinically useful index of psychological well-being and prognosis: A brief report," *Psychotherapy: Theory, Research, Practice, Training* 45, no. 2 (2008): 268–72.

17. Psalm 126:5.

18. Bava Batra 60b.

Acknowledgments

In few places in my professional life has the core Jewish value of interdependence been more evident than in the writing of this book. While every single mistake is mine, I am grateful to dozens of people who made it possible for this book to come to my life.

The first, deepest, and greatest appreciation goes to Rabbi Avigayil Halpern, who served as my chevruta, research assistant, rebbe, and rabbi through the writing of the book. Her deep, traditional, radical Torah weaves its way throughout, well beyond the places where she is quoted verbatim.

I also want to thank the students and congregants of Sixth & I Historic Synagogue in Washington, DC. Eleven years of teaching the Jewish Welcome Workshop, the Interfaith Couples Workshop, and so many other classes formed the wellsprings from which this content grew. Thank you for being curious, vulnerable, headstrong, loving, and willing to learn. I'm eternally grateful for all you taught me. And to all the other Jewish communities I've served: Congregation Kol Ami (Boca Raton), Congregation Kesher Shalom (Abington, Pennsylvania), the Jewish Federation of Greater Philadelphia, National Women's Philanthropy of the Jewish Federations of North America, and all of the various Next Gen cohorts—thank you for inspiring me and pushing me to grow.

And to my new family, the Aspen Jewish Congregation, thank you for being warm and welcoming. I can't wait to see what we build together.

To my Editor with a capital E, Batya Rosenblum, who found *Chutzpod!* among millions of podcasts, who has been my cheerleader throughout, and who, in editing this book, found at least one halachic mistake: Thank you. To all the pre-readers of this book: I am especially grateful to Rabbi Elyse Seidner-Joseph, Rabbi Adam Zeff, and rabbinical student Hilary Cohen, who edited the minutiae and pushed back on some of the big questions. And to all the others who read and commented: Elisheva Goldberg, Jodi Kantor, Rabbi Scott Perlo, Rabbi Aaron Potek, Russell Shaw, and Suzanne Stutman: Thank you.

I count the creation of Sefaria.org to be as important as the invention of the printing press. Thank you to everyone who brought this miracle of Jewish learning to life. This book absolutely would not exist without the website you created.

This book was written primarily in two locations: the planes and lounges of United Airlines, as I flew back and forth to the Roaring Fork Valley of Colorado, and the offices of the Aviv Foundation, in Washington, DC. I am deeply grateful to Chani and Steve Laufer; the executive director, Adam Simon; and the entire Aviv team for offering me encouragement and office space in which to research and write.

To all the rabbis who taught me over the years: all the teachers at the Charles E Smith Jewish Day School, especially Rabbi Harold Bell (z"l) and Rabbi Jan Caryl Kaufman; the rabbis and teachers of Adas Israel past and present, especially Michael Stern (z"l) and Rabbi Avis Miller; the rabbis and teachers of the Wexner Foundation, especially Rabbi Elka Abrahamson; the rabbis and teachers of the Reconstructionist Rabbinical College, especially Tamar Kamionkowski, Rabbi David Teutsch, Rabbi Sarra Lev, Rabbi Linda Holtzman, and Rabbi Joel Hecker. Thank you. I was watching and learning all along.

I don't even know how to begin to thank my rabbinic colleagues, all the members of class fourteen, and my dear friends. I live in fear that I will leave someone out, so rather than make a list, know this: If we have stayed up late into the night talking, or crying from joy or sadness, know that I love you—and thank you.

I have been blessed with an extraordinary family, both nuclear and extended. To all the Goldbergs, Singers, Andresses, and Stutmans: Thank you for holding me in the terrible moments and celebrating with me in the wonderful ones. And to my brothers, Zak and Gabe, and sister-in-law Anne, I adore you; thank you for letting me regress from time to time and not being too annoyed. And thanks for Herschel and Mary Mom. My parents, Ned (z"l) and Suzanne privileged Jewish education—mine, my brothers', and their own—above just about all else. This book is one result of their commitment. To lose a father and then gain a stepfather like Jon Wilkenfeld, who comes complete with some of the best stepfamily around, is an unexpected and true gift. And to Caleb, Ma'ayan, and Natalia, who model softness and strength, joy and honesty, growth and loyalty—I love you more than you could possibly understand, except perhaps if one day you choose to have children of your own.

And to Rusty: We knew on our second date that we had found the one our hearts desired. Thank you for always letting me follow my dreams. I can't wait to see what you build next.

About the Author

RABBI SHIRA STUTMAN is a nationally known faith-based leader and change maker with more than twenty years of experience motivating and inspiring groups large and small. She is the senior rabbi of the Aspen Jewish Congregation and co-host of the top-ranked PRX podcast *Chutzpod!* in which she provides Jewish answers to life's contemporary questions and help listeners build lives of meaning. She also teaches Torah and speaks nationally on topics that include growing welcoming Jewish spiritual communities; building the connective tissues between different types of people; and the current American Jewish community zeitgeist. As founder of Mixed Multitudes, a consultancy that exposes diverse groups of Jews and fellow travelers to the beauty and power of Jewish life, tradition, and conversation, she currently is working on a variety of projects: running programs that support Jews in having less reactive and more heart-centered conversations about Israel; teaching in progressive institutions about antisemitism; and serving as scholar-in-residence for projects that build the next generation of philanthropic leadership. She was the founding rabbi of Sixth & I Historic Synagogue in Washington, DC, in addition to a number of other start-up Jewish life initiatives.

mixedmultitudes.net | ⃝ shirastutman | ⬜ Rabbi Shira Stutman